SUMMONING GENIUS:

A MIDLIFE GUIDE TO DISCOVERING IDENTITY, MEANING AND PURPOSE

BEN HUMMELL LPC, LMFT

Cover design by Nick Zelinger, NZ Graphics
Interior layout by Veronica Yager, YellowStudios

ISBN: 978-0-9971616-0-1
Library of Congress Control Number: 2015960724

*To my sweet soul partner whose
loving presence fills my heart with smiles.*

I love you.

Acknowledgments

With or without their knowing, the following people have helped me write this book. I wish to thank and honor them for the difference they have made in my life.

Laura Rose for her loving support and encouragement (and book title!).

Brennan Anderson, my son, for allowing me to encourage his genius callings.

Dr. Lorell Frysh, my Murshida and friend, for the depth of her patience and wisdom.

Beverly McLaughlin, my sister, for never giving up on me.

Sasha Edwards for her true friendship.

Colibri Montalvo, my soul daughter, for her strength and love.

Tamar Gellar for helping me to remember my strength.

Marlo Dalby for our soul friendship.

Lila Harding for sharing her genius muse.

Suzanne Mark for her great kindness.

Will Allen for sharing his creative energy and example.

Dr. Dan Sternberg for his gentle and loving advice.

Sanaya Roman for her friendship and guidance.

CONTENTS

FOREWORD

The purpose of this book is to provoke a response in readers. It is a call to action. It is intended to stir the pot and create new possibilities and opportunities in lives that may have become stagnant. Its message to readers is to challenge the personal status quo at midlife by uncovering the talents and abilities that they, as individuals, have been born to express.

This book presents ideas, exercises, and encouragement for the second half of life, where many of us have dropped off the map creatively and expressively. Its task is to help the reader uncover the wealth of his or her character, which, by midlife, has been deepened through lived experience and which, I propose, has value greater than gold, regardless of what form or shape it has taken.

Using an ancient idea regarding the source of our greatest qualities, namely the *Genius spirit* with which each of us were born, this book serves as a mirror, provocateur, companion, and guide to the discovery process.

The midlife period is a crucial time to become reinvigorated through a reconnection with your creative possibilities, because, by this time, you may have become disenchanted by your successes as well as your failures and have a need to find something genuinely yours that brings a fresh breeze of possibility to your life experience going forward. This book proposes that that something already exists as an underutilized part of you that can be uncovered and engaged, and that this largely forgotten part can provide rich and fertile ground for growing into more of what you are to become here, in this life.

Midlife is not a time to roll over and play dead. Much of life has yet to be lived, and if you're reading this, you know that this is true; you can feel it in your marrow, perhaps as a faint calling, or perhaps as a loud and insistent voice of urgency.

As you move through the ideas on these pages, some may resonate with you more than others, but my sincere hope is that this book will serve as a much-needed wake up call to those of you who are currently sensing the genuine inherent human need for continued life growth and expansion of expression.

While we are still here, the more that we can uncover our natural and unique callings, the more we can offer to those whom we love as well as to people we may never meet who may benefit from the gifts we have brought to this life to develop and share.

May you use this book in that spirit and, in turn, allow what you uncover in yourself to become an encouragement for others to answer their deepest callings.

What Is Genius, Really?

In modern times, namely the last 100 years or so, the term *Genius* has been associated with the I.Q., or *intelligence quotient* of a person, which is the score someone gets on a standardized test originally developed by French psychologist Alfred Binet. He designed the test to predict how successfully any given student would perform in school. More recent and contemporary versions of this test propose that if someone scores above a 140, they fall into the genius range of intelligence, when compared to others who don't score as highly on the same test. Geniuses are considered to be more gifted or special than others, and therefore, a distance is placed between them and the lower IQed masses.

Historically, though, the word *Genius* had a different meaning and significance. Stemming from the Latin words *gignere* (to beget or produce) and *gigno* (the superior or divine nature in everything), a person's Genius was defined as a guiding spirit that accompanies the soul when each person is born. Everyone has one. This spirit is imbued with specific talents, attributes, and creative leanings that make it unique—one of a kind—and therefore precious and intrinsically valuable. All of these specific and unique qualities are seen as gifts that are brought to share with the world.

Each Genius is actually a Genius seed, containing all of the attributes of the mature plant *in potential.* Given the right circumstances, the seed can grow into its full expression, bearing the fruits and fragrances that it is meant to give outwardly to the world as gifts. The task of all of us human beings, then, is to allow our Genius to integrate into our everyday lives so that those gifts can be given, resulting in a felt sense of fulfillment for each of us. Conversely, the belief in Genius held that if those gifts aren't given, they may begin to stagnate within us, and this stagnation can manifest in both physical and psychological symptoms in our lives.

Psychologist James Hillman explains the terms used historically for the Genius in us:

> For centuries we have searched for the right term for this "call." The Romans named it your *genius;* the Greeks, your *daimon;* and the Christians, your guardian angel. . . . The Neoplatonists referred to it as an imaginal body, the *ochema,* that carried you like a vehicle. It was your personal bearer or support.

According to Hillman's account, rather than being a one-in-a-million phenomenon, Genius is actually universal in nature. Everyone's makeup contains a Genius, which is to a greater or lesser extent recognized, realized, or given expression by the individual. Regardless of what type of uniqueness the Genius in you has carried here, its desire is to be brought out and to be allowed to express its own tones and flavors.

Genius is also seen as a guardian spirit or angel. But the traditional concept of a guardian angel evokes images of our physical protection against evil or dangerous circumstances, whereas Genius's role in our lives is to bear responsibility for keeping our uniqueness alive; it protects our innate qualities, talents, and gifts from becoming lost or diluted. It serves us by reminding us in various ways and throughout the entirety of our lives of our personal life callings and the things we were meant to do that will instill individual meaning and purpose. It provides us with both physical and psychological symptoms as indicators of how and when we are ignoring this essential part of ourselves, and where to look for and allow our Genius expression to emerge and manifest. From the time of our birth until our physical death, it continues to care for us in the form of keeping the fire of our creative potential alive by sheltering its flame against the elements of forgetfulness, opposition, and discouragement. Genius's protection thus extends to the depths of the inner blueprints of our life that were provided to us when we were born. Genius holds us to the universal mandate we are each given to discover and express what those blueprints hold. Some divine architect has made a unique set of these plans for each of us, and the construction and expression of it can be carried out only by the individual who holds them in his or her existential marrow. Our genius knows this and, through a myriad of inner and outer experiences, consistently reminds us of what we individually came here to do.

We can reciprocate our Genius's care and protection by first acknowledging its presence and then by making time to see that we give it the opportunity to shine. As Hillman puts it, "once upon a time what took such good care of me was a guardian spirit, and I damn well knew how to pay it appropriate attention."

Throughout this book, I sometimes refer to Genius as the *Genius spirit*, or *our innate Genius, our guardian spirit*, or simply *Genius*. You may want to take notice of how many times the word Genius will trigger a mental connotation of the contemporary "I.Q." definition of Genius and observe any accompanying feelings that may arise, ranging from the self-doubt that you even have Genius qualities, to feelings of superiority from singling yourself out as special because of your Genius traits. Remember that these qualities are unique in each of us; every human being who ever was and ever will be born has their own. Most things in the world are identified as being special and unique because of their rarity and limited quantity. So it is with our individual Genius. It expresses a particular flavor only once, and that is through a particular one of us as we are and as we grow and live. There is absolutely no need to compare or compete with anyone regarding Genius, because living our Genius has at its root a singular historical opportunity for expression.

For the sake of illustrating the Genius qualities appearing in an individual, let's turn to someone commonly seen by others as a Genius, namely Albert Einstein. The reason for using such a globally known figure who has obviously contributed a great deal to our scientific culture as an example is because of what Einstein had to say about his particular Genius and how he regarded creativity and calling in the lives of other individuals as well. The most remarkable things about his life aren't necessarily his scientific theories and discoveries but rather his innate character that valued, above all else, imagination, creativity, and intuition. It seems that in order for Einstein to conceive, develop, and present his theories, he first had to give the insatiable curiosity innate in his Genius a great amount of latitude and range to express itself.

> "The true sign of intelligence is not knowledge but the imagination."
> — *Albert Einstein*

An example such as Einstein is not meant to be idolized and imitated but to be seen as an individual who listened to his unique Genius and made more and more space for it to come to fruition in his life.

The Importance of Finding Genius at Midlife

For those of us who, by midlife, haven't been actively living with Genius as a major contributor in our life expressions, the time is ripe to turn our attention to it. With the exception of childhood, there is no more important time to begin the effort than at this crucial stage when the deep existential questions appear, and the need for life meaning and purpose becomes a primary concern.

One thing to know is that it is a natural phenomenon to begin to question our life decisions and choices that have brought us to this point. The pendulum of life can only swing in one direction just so far before it needs to move in the exact opposite direction. The first half of life is about pushing to create a space for ourselves in a difficult world full of competition and scarcity. We are preoccupied with achievement and its shadowy twin: the fear of loss. Our identities are created by what we do and who we are in the eyes of others. We are living an outer life without the depth that comes from the integration of our Genius qualities. Even those who discover part of their Genius at an early age and have actively expressed it will still have other Genius qualities that are necessary to bring out at midlife, due to the pendulum nature of our psychological development. No one escapes the need to engage consciously in this "return" to these innate qualities of Genius, but many live the second half of their lives suffering due to misunderstanding the call of their Genius spirit to once again engage in their childlike explorations and creative leanings.

Something Is Missing

A common symptom at midlife is the incessant feeling that something is missing from our life experience. We may make numerous and often desperate attempts to fill this empty space by acquiring possessions, achievements, or lovers, but to no avail. This is normal, and the important thing is what happens after we try and fail to fill our inner void with these things.

The felt need for something more, or the feeling that we are missing something doesn't come from nowhere and isn't simply the whining of an entitled child. This feeling is actually set into motion by something very real that has dwelled within our existential identities from the time we were born: our inbuilt Genius qualities that have something genuine and important to express. When we have ignored this calling for a great deal of time, and because our Genius has its own agenda in our lives, it will make itself known through these feelings of discontent that arise in us. If our Genius wasn't there within us from the beginning, there would not be a problem with our life experiences as they are. They would be enough, and we wouldn't feel any need to change anything. Because we do feel this need, especially at midlife, we have a natural mandate to engage with the thing that is speaking to us through our symptoms and feelings of incompleteness.

As we go through different stages of physical and psychological development as children, the milestones can be detected fairly easily in the development of speech, locomotion, and cognitive acuity. Several well-known developmental theories are generally believed to be at least partially true by many professionals whose fields require them to study and observe human development. One such theory developed by psychologist Erik Erikson may be helpful as an illustration of finding our Genius at midlife. Erikson identified seven stages of human psychological development that generally occur at certain ages of physical growth. The stage that interests us here is the one that Erikson named Generativity vs. Stagnation, which takes place between the ages of 40 and 65.

Generativity vs. Stagnation is the stage when, according to Erikson, we settle down, raise families, contribute to our communities, and develop a sense of our individual role in larger society. When this stage is reached and its attributes are attained, says Erikson, the individual is generative and engaged in work, family, and community. This *generativity* brings a sense of identity and place, providing a person with an individual sense of life meaning and purpose. On the other hand, if one fails to be generative and all of the aspects of this stage aren't being experienced, one experiences *stagnation*, usually accompanied by feelings of worthlessness, confusion, dissatisfaction, and an emptiness in one's life.

Luckily for us humans, a felt sense of stagnation can be as good as an alarm clock, wake-up call, or call to action. And fortunately for us, stagnation itself goes against the basic nature of our innate Genius. Through these feelings of emptiness and lost purpose, our Genius begins to let us know that it's time for us to pay attention to its messages. Symptoms are part of the language of Genius. It speaks existentially in images, dreams, and inner experience. Some of its messages are translated as suffering and pain simply because we're misunderstanding their larger meaning. If there were no Genius in us desiring to be brought out into the world to be expressed, there would be no problem with stagnation. Stagnation would be just fine as an experience, and we wouldn't feel that anything else was needed.

As I am writing this, sitting in front of my fireplace in the early morning, I am having some trouble with my firewood. I have had to start my fire several times, repositioning the logs, adding kindling, and blowing on the embers in order to get the wood to catch. The fire has stagnated, and it has taken my effort and conscious attention to assist and allow the potentiality of the wood to provide heat for me. The effort on my part makes me a deliberate participant in the transformation of a dead tree into a living source of light and heat. My sense and feeling of being physically cold is the motivation, and the calling is from the stagnated potential in the wood to do something about it. By listening and responding, using a combination of a developed skill and creativity, and after some trial and error, I have managed to help some dry wood express a transformation into living energy. The amount of light and heat it is giving is exponentially more than the effort I've made to let it happen.

So it is with Genius. If we pay attention to its call, and respond with careful attention, giving it the proper conditions to express its uniqueness, it can release its energy that has been waiting in potential, which, in turn, will manifest as meaning and purpose in our lives.

Our Changing Sense of Value

"Nature's first green is gold,
Her hardest hue to hold.
Her early leaf's a flower;
But only so an hour.
Then leaf subsides to leaf.
So Eden sank to grief,
So dawn goes down to day.
Nothing gold can stay."
— *Robert Frost*

Part of our psychological state when we reach midlife centers around the fact that our bodies are aging and around all of the challenges that come along with that aging process. No one is ready to get old. Psychologically, it is a rare person who moves from one stage of life to another completely prepared and accepting of the physical changes that take place over a lifetime. For most of us, reaching midlife comes as somewhat of a shock, and we may feel a legion of emotions when confronting the evidence before us that the first half of our life is over. Like being born naked and vulnerable as a baby, we now find ourselves in a similar position in that the illusion of immortality and invulnerability we felt as adolescents and young adults has given way to a newer reality that presents a glimpse of the finality of our lives. This is why midlife elicits existential anxiety and deeper questing. Being faced with a realization of our own mortality tends to make us think about larger, more universal issues that we may have neglected to face up until now.

Robert Frost's poem has a sense of wistful sadness regarding the nature of the "gold" in our lives leaving us. Just when we've come to appreciate it, the gold has gone, having turned into another color before our very eyes. There is a value placed on the symbol of gold for youth that is not replaced by a symbol of greater value by midlife, especially in modern cultures. This is why the idea of midlife, instead of being celebrated as a graduation from a state of inexperience into a state of maturity, is often experienced as a tragic loss of the only thing that is seen as valuable: the gold of our youth. The real tragedy however, is the lack of recognition of the transformation of that gold.

Energy is never lost; it just changes form and goes on. Our life energy is no exception. Although it may seem as if we have lost our youth and all of the entitlements that went along with it, our life energy remains as vital as ever. We just have to be able to recognize the new form it has taken as we journey into midlife.

The tendency of wanting things to stay the same in our lives is something that everyone without exception will have to confront and challenge. Midlife is a particularly auspicious time to engage in this challenge. The illusion of having unlimited time has begun to erode, exposing the reality that we have no say in how much time we have left. This realization can lead to feelings of helplessness, anxiety, and depression. But if we can review our lives up until now in terms of the changes that have already occurred and what they have produced, we can see that midlife is simply the next place and time for something different to take place on the stage of our life experience.

The changing nature of things is indeed a universally shared predicament. If we understand that transformations of all kinds are part of the human experience, we will be able to welcome the physical and psychological seasons as they come and go, accepting their gifts as they appear in the current of time. The extent to which we have learned to accept and even embrace change is the key to being able to navigate our midlife journey successfully.

Change Tolerance Inventory

- Has anything changed in your life recently?
- Name your first reaction to this change.
- Have you reacted to previous life changes in a similar way?
- Did this reaction keep the change from happening?
- What did you lose as a result of the change?
- Name something that you have gained because of this change happening.
- Has this change brought any unsuspected insights about yourself and your life?
- What advice would you give to someone else if they were experiencing this same life change?

Write down your answers to these questions and see if you can recognize a pattern to how you have learned to deal with life changes. Consider whether if this pattern actually serves the purpose of helping you to accept and move through your life changes or if there is something about it that isn't working. You can then use these insights to do something different when you are faced with future changes that may come along.

The Potency of a Symbol

If we wish for success in inviting the tremendous personal growth that can occur at midlife, we will need to embrace a new paradigm for living the second half of our lives — one that has as its symbol something more precious than gold. As we become more comfortable with the knowledge that all of physical life is ephemeral and that we can use the time we still have to create a more meaningful existence, we begin to value things that invigorate, energize, and mobilize us. We have no time to waste in inertia; there is still much of our Genius to express and explore while we are still here.

It is important to have a symbol that represents the totality of our experience. A symbol for a quest or journey should embody a distillation or concentration of the qualities we see as valuable and want to bring out in ourselves. This symbol is a focal point or mandala to return to again and again in order to center our focus and intent. It serves as inspiration us to keep going when our enthusiasm has waned and as an energy source from which to recharge and invigorate our existential batteries.

For your midlife journey, I invite you to choose any symbol that deeply resonates with you and your life experience. For my personal journey, I have chosen the symbol of the Dragonfly as the embodiment of the evolution of our lost gold. In many cultures, the Dragonfly stands for increased self-realization and greater maturity. Its habit of flying over the surface of water symbolizes the quality of looking past outward appearances into the deeper aspects hidden beneath the surface of things. Dragonflies are born in water but then rise as they mature and instead use the air to navigate their world. They represent the evolution of consciousness through transformation and rebirth. The Dragonfly is able to fly in all six directions effortlessly and change direction in an instant. This is the agility and elegance that can only come from maturity and experience. In the second half of our lives, we can approach our challenges with an agile awareness that has ripened through years of trial, error, and experiment. The dragonfly's body is iridescent; it can show literally all colors of the spectrum, depending on the angle of the light that falls upon it. As we uncover and express our Genius qualities at midlife, we can use the unique colors we discover in ourselves to respond creatively to whatever situation comes our way. We now possess a large vocabulary of experience with which to address whatever self-created illusions attempt to block our progress on the road of individuation.

The dragonfly has another important quality, in that it can see a 360-degree circumference around itself because of the way its eyes are formed. This characteristic symbolizes the wisdom inherent in midlife Genius expression and the ability to use our vision from our vantage point as mature individuals to see farther than the limits of our self-involvement in a still-forming identity. If we take advantage of how the lessons of experience have "opened our eyes," we can use our Dragonfly quality of seeing ourselves more deeply and clearly.

Perhaps the most valuable quality that the dragonfly symbolizes is the ability to see through self-made illusions. The process of what we experience at midlife, and certainly our task of uncovering our Genius qualities, requires that we exercise our ability to see ourselves clearly — the good, the bad, the dark and light — all at once, without judgment or fear. Self-made illusions are the most difficult of all to see, because the previous versions of our identities are wrapped up in them. This previous identity is like a house of cards, which for many of us, by midlife, has been blown into an unrecognizable heap by the winds of time. Remember that the Dragonfly lives in the water as a nymph for the first part of its life before it takes to the air as its natural habitat. The dragonfly symbolizes the strength, wisdom, creativity, and flexibility to allow a newer and more genuine identity to emerge — one that is based on an experiential reality through which we have already lived, rather than the uninformed, blind quest for an illusory and idealistic version of ourselves that we embarked upon in our youth.

Seeing through our own illusions is really the single most valuable quality to develop at midlife, because without it, we are consigned to running on the proverbial hamster wheel, repeating the same actions over and over and being confused as to why we experience the same unrewarding outcomes. The dragonfly, with its color, speed, and grace, exemplifies the creative resourcefulness that is needed to make the journey past the version of ourselves that we have outgrown. Its quest is deliberate and purposeful. It has no more time to waste dwelling in the past. It recognizes that life is happening right now.

Midlife Growth

One of the last realizations of those experiencing a midlife transitional period is that something natural is occurring in them. One of the aims of this book is to normalize the growth process in midlife in order to help those experiencing it to cooperate with what is happening within them instead of fighting with it.

It is natural for anyone in midlife to want to resist any changes that seem to be occurring. Changes are happening in our bodies, manifesting as more limited ranges of motion in our movements, various illnesses that may show up, the mental and emotional realization that there is a limited amount of time left to live our lives, and the ultimate confrontation on a soul level with the reality of eventual physical death. At one point in our lives, we need to be confronted with these new feelings and symptoms that are intended to motivate us once again to move, change, and grow. Physical changes and limitations remind us to take care of the physical body-houses we've been given to live in while on this earthly adventure. Mental and emotional changes take place in order to motivate us to change old and outdated modes of perception that no longer serve our new stage of growth at midlife. The realization of the certainty of physical death serves to help us to enjoy and use each day we are given to enrich our own lives with the things that bring us meaning and purpose, in turn affecting the lives of others that we touch along the way.

Most people are aware of the word *crisis* associated with the word midlife. This pairing of words was first used in a paper by the Canadian psychoanalyst Elliot Jaques, who was 48 at the time of its publication. The two words are rarely seen without one another these days and are associated with a time of confusion, struggle, and corresponding feelings of being lost in the world. It is important to note that after this publication, Jaques went on to write 12 books, marry, form a consulting company with his wife, and contribute to the field of psychology for the next 38 years! This "second life" lived by the person describing a crisis points to the fact that *crisis* must have had a different meaning for him—one that contained not only danger, difficulty, and trouble but also possibility and promise.

The word *crisis* has at its root two Greek words: *krisis,* meaning decision, judgment, choice, and *krino,* to choose or decide. So, as with any turning point in our lives, one aspect of life is ending while another begins. This new beginning, heralded by *krisis* or *krino,* is thus a time for a decision and a choice. Free will is deeply involved in this decision, and it is at this point when we can call on our latent Genius qualities to come to our aid and inform this very important choice we are compelled to make. This choice or decision is actually the choice to live or to die, metaphorically. We may either dwell and stagnate in our previously lived version of life that has brought us this far or move in pace with life itself into the next chapter and incarnation where fresh possibility exists.

Although a crisis can signal danger and the need to make a decision, it is important to recognize this crossroads as a naturally occurring phenomenon in a time of growth and development. The changes happening in the time period between our mid-30s and mid-60s is therefore referred to here as *midlife growth,* a term that sheds a more accurate light on what is actually taking place. The commonly held idea of a crisis is only one side of the equation. Crisis in the advent of midlife is merely the motivation provided to us to make the changes that will ultimately lead to a greater sense and expression of our individual and innate life purpose.

There is a teaching story which depicts a teacher and a student standing inside a building with high windows. They observe that a pigeon has become trapped inside the building and is confused as to how to get out. The pigeon has become exhausted from its attempts to find its way to freedom and is despondently perched on a shelf on the wall. The teacher approaches the bird and quite suddenly and loudly claps his hands. The bird, responding to what it perceives as a threat to its life, instinctually flies away through an open window into the welcoming sunlight.

The student remarks, "See how quickly the bird found his way out with your intervention!" To which the teacher replies, "Yes, and see how the bird thought that this was an act that meant to do him harm. The motivation for it to free itself had come from experiencing something that felt contrary to his freedom and possibly even life threatening. Until of course, he flew out of an open window into the limitless freedom of the sky."

In order to experience midlife as a growth process, we will need to see whatever is happening to us as an impetus for changing our life approach. Just as the pigeon in the story had exhausted itself trying to escape its imprisonment using its old methods, we try to employ methods of living that have worked before in our younger lives. That was a time for pushing forward, forging trails, and making a mark on the world by the exercise of sheer will. The time of Midlife Growth, however, is a time of responding to life's cues cooperatively. Something inside of us wants us to grow and change in order to continue our journey. This is a time of seeing our limitations simply as boulders in the stream of our lives against which we initially crash but ultimately flow around in any way we can to continue down the stream. The boulders are not there to stop us but to engage us in a life-giving play of creativity that generates energy and opens up opportunities to see ourselves differently than before. If there is anything that is required for a fruitful period of Midlife Growth to take place, it is the willingness to see ourselves in a new way. This can be a frightening prospect when approached from the crisis side of the equation. But if we encounter the crisis willingly, realizing the need to change our basic perceptions of ourselves for the sake of moving with the flow of life again, we are energized and excited at the prospect. We become explorers of our own consciousness, which engenders new experiences through which we learn about ourselves as individuals. Our growth and development continues until our physical death and, depending on our particular viewpoint, possibly even beyond that.

Course Corrections

Mythologist and author Michael Meade, in discussing Genius, uses an analogy of a boat on the water to illustrate the conditions of our moving through life. He explains that a boat is never really on course, as it is consistently being blown off course by changing winds and sea currents, and that the helmsman is steering the boat by constantly correcting the course of the boat toward the direction he is heading.

This deliberate participation in the minutiae of the journey engages the helmsman to be consciously awake and alive in his task. The wind provides the needed energy for the journey, and the course corrections he makes always point in the direction of his destination.

Embracing the idea that our life, like a boat on the sea, is always off course and in need of consistent corrective steering can be a difficult proposition. As Aristotle postulated centuries ago, nature abhors a vacuum. In my experience, it seems as if nature also abhors a straight line. We would like to believe that we can set a course and continue straight ahead in one direction in order to meet our goals and aspirations. However, if we can look back at our lives and remember the different experiences we've had, we will see that almost without exception, the plans that we made invariably changed due to unforeseen events that took place. The fact is that the necessity of course corrections makes our lives deep and interesting. The processes that we must go through in order to make those corrections change and transform us into more authentic people.

By the time midlife rolls around, most of us are due for a significant course correction. Sometimes, when we get a moment of rest from running the daily operations of our life-ship and actually look up at the horizon, we say, "Where am I? How did I get here? Where am I heading?"

We've been sailing without steering for such a long while that it can actually be quite surprising and disturbing when we finally pick our heads up to look out at where we are. Many times, we find that we are living a life that we just sort of fell into out of necessity, convenience, or habit and that we're not actually living the life we want to live. We may find ourselves in a job we hate, experiencing health problems from lack of exercise or bad eating habits, having an addiction to alcohol or drugs, or going through a divorce or depression. All of these things are possibilities at midlife, and it is exactly at this point that we can become psychologically sober with the bracing realization that we are not where or who we want to be. With a type of existential sobriety, we can begin again to steer the ship of our life on a desirable course and consciously choose where we want to go. This time we will know that course corrections are normal, everyday occurrences and that what engages us to act keeps us vital and alive.

Midlife Imagination

Everything we see around us made by humans was originally an image in someone's mind. As a craftsman who built furniture for more than 25 years, I was constantly amazed while looking at a dresser or cabinet I had completed because I knew that it was originally just an idea and a picture in my head! How did this object get here? Even though I had gone through the process of building the dresser or cabinet piece by piece, a disconnect occurred once the work was done and what had existed only in fantasy was sitting there completed in front of me. It always felt like some sort of magical occurrence.

Genius at work in our lives operates in the same way. Our Genius spirit provides us with images, inclinations, and motivations for specific things that are uniquely ours to express. These things have their OWN desire to be manifested in the world regardless of whether we've listened to their messages up until now. Think about that for a second. Our Genius has its OWN desire to manifest things. We, living as separate, ego-oriented people, especially in Western culture, operate under the assumption that we are on our own as individuals striving for some sort of success against all odds in a hostile world. Now, imagine that there is actually something very real inside of us, constantly calling and motivating us to express things that will bring us the fulfillment that we naturally crave. Something is already providing the imaginal images and impulses necessary to be creatively happy, and this thing is actually in complete congruence with the universe. Things *want* to happen through us. This Genius is actually pulling us toward these things as much as we are making the effort to go toward them. The Genius never stops sending its messages to us; it is operating under its organic functioning in doing so. Humans seem to lose connection to this instinct somewhere along the way. When we see someone following the messages of their Genius, it may appear that they are acting in an impractical or even foolish way, spending their time building an ark or studying an ancient, dead language that no one speaks any more. But following the breadcrumbs that have been left by our Genius is a true and intelligent way to participate with a part of ourselves that has been largely ignored by modern man.

Participation with our Genius spirit usually begins with paying attention to our unique fantasies and imaginings and taking their promises of freedom and fulfillment seriously. Following societal norms, we have accepted such things such as bank accounts and material consumption as important aspects of our lives while ignoring our inborn tendencies, which only by our living them out in our daily lives can bring us the fulfillment we attempt to get from the "practical" things.

This is not to say that while living in a society we don't need to pay the mortgage, take care of our family and our health, or contribute in some way to our communities. It's just that without giving any attention to our innate Genius, we're living without the imaginal and creative sustenance and nourishment that has been ours potentially since birth. This type of sustenance cannot be had by climbing social ladders of success or by being famous for the sake of being famous; instead, it is had by recovering our inner integrity, which stems from listening and embodying our innate Genius nature. This nature never needs to be created but rather just listened to and left to unfold naturally in our lives.

If Not Now, When?

The fallacy that midlife is the beginning of our slow descent into old age and death, with all of our glory days and opportunities behind us, can be extinguished by each of us with the help of our Genius guardian spirit. There are countless examples of people who have continued being creative and expressive throughout their entire lives. Some of them are known by their contributions/gifts to the world, but most are unknown except to the few that they have touched. Each one of these souls has come to the realization that there is literally no time left to hem and haw about their futures. A desperate desire for a deep sense of life purpose and Genius expression has pushed them beyond the self-imposed limitations of earlier life. They see the opportunity for a further unfolding of their life story as happening right now in the immediacy of this very moment. Whatever opportunity serves as the impetus for growth and change is quickly welcomed; great energy is released along with the shedding of our illusions about our limited options and possibilities.

Stepping into a creatively active midlife from whichever point on the chronological arc we happen to find ourselves is the key to acknowledging that our Genius has work to do and things to express. To forsake the false modesty of not wanting to call attention to ourselves out of the fear of seeming egotistical and selfish and to actually provide space for the uniqueness of our Genius expression to take place is the ultimate act of selflessness in this event and results in genuine giving and caring. Seeing things from this angle may necessitate a paradigm shift for many of us who have been used to taking an apologetic stance regarding the things we have to express to the world. This is a particularly auspicious and sacred event—a rebirth and revisioning of our lives. It is an initiation into a new perception of our world that changes everything. Where there once were the walls and limitations of our younger lives' failures, there are now signs indicating new pathways to follow. Where there were walls and ceilings built of past discouragements, there are now windows, doors, and the open sky of possibility and promise. These vistas appear upon the death of our young adulthood, just as new leaves appear on a palm tree as the old ones die and fall away.

SUMMONING GENIUS | 21

Someday

As a young boy, one of the most soul-crushing experiences was when I heard my father repeat his favorite two words to me: "We'll see."

"Can we play catch tonight when you get home from work, Dad?"

"We'll see."

"Will you come to my baseball game this Saturday?"

"We'll see."

"Can you help me with my homework this weekend?"

"We'll see."

You can see where this is going. All of these "we'll see"s had the postponement until "someday" stamped on the back of them. For a child with a raging Genius spirit, this was consistent and systematic torture. I eventually learned that "someday" never comes and that I couldn't afford to postpone being creative and expressive by waiting for anyone or anything.

As children, we have no idea that there is something else that wants to express itself through us. Our Genius spirit has a creative agenda, carrying with it the energy required to achieve and express this creativity. This energy indeed "calls" to us, sending us signs and portents about what it wants to express, and manifests in us as attractions, inspirations, fascinations, and fixations on particular things. It may instill a passion for painting, mentoring, mountain climbing, or writing or a fascination with cooking, building, or business. The Genius has no limit to what it finds important to express, but express it must. The expression of our Genius talents is always now. By the time midlife comes around, heeding the call of Genius can be likened to taking a life-sustaining breath, and its insistence on not waiting a moment longer to be allowed to emerge is indeed its gift to us.

We have all bought into the "someday" trick to some extent and may have even adopted it to postpone indefinitely many pursuits that could have provided skills, knowledge, and insight and expanded our horizons. By midlife however, the reality is clear: the only thing that will happen "someday" is death. At midlife, there is literally no more time to waste, and no excuses are good enough. Every day counts at this point. We are faced with an energy-producing dilemma: start living and expressing our unique Genius qualities now or continue on the expressionless road to our eventual death. How fortunate are we.

Midlife Signals

Midlife is a time when the results of our past decisions begin to manifest in our inner and outer life experience. Regrets for things we have and haven't done begin to break through the surface of our consciousness as thoughts and feelings. Qualities of our Genius that have gone unexpressed begin to manifest in the form of a disturbance of some kind, either psychological or physical. This disruption is often the last avenue for our Genius to break through our well-worn habitual thinking and unconscious patterns of behavior and express itself. Many times, in order to change something and correct our life course, we somehow need to be shaken out of a midlife stupor. We have become expert somnambulists and need to be awakened by something outside the norm. Nothing grabs our attention

> "A man is born gentle and weak. At his death he is hard and stiff. Green plants are tender and filled with sap. At their death they are withered and dry. Therefore the stiff and unbending is the disciple of death. The gentle and yielding is the disciple of life."
>
> — *Lao Tsu*

like being suddenly presented with a challenging situation. Swiss psychiatrist and psychotherapist Carl Jung says that "when an inner situation is not made conscious, it appears outside as fate." Many fateful events have heralded significant changes and new beginnings for people, simply by presenting an opportunity to change something that has become so habitual that it is no longer helping or serving us as it had before, earlier in life.

If life is always in a state of flux, it follows that anything we do in the same way for a long, long time is an action or thought pattern that has become a frozen and brittle thing, is no longer in the flow of life, and no longer has the capability to adapt, change, and respond to challenges that arise. Midlife is a time of letting go of what no longer works. But in order to do so, in most cases, we must have a disturbance or difficulty that presents an opportunity for real change. The following story illustrates the need to change our old habits that simply cannot navigate a situation that demands a new, creative response from us.

Two friends went on an adventure through the wilderness and started out by taking their canoe up a beautiful river. There were long stretches of calm water alternating with fast moving rapids that challenged them to respond in each moment. At every new turn in the river, their trusty canoe rose to the occasion with steadiness and balance, and carried them through each calm and turbulent passage.

One day, as they paddled their canoe, they noticed that the river was becoming increasingly narrow and shallow until they eventually came to a place where the water flowed into an opening in the ground. Beyond that point, there was only a forest thick with trees and underbrush. The friends, in order to continue their journey, decided to carry their canoe on their heads and hike through the woods that lay before them. Since the trees were so many, and there was no worn path on which to walk, the friends were having an incredibly difficult time, and were making little progress forward.

Finally, they met an inhabitant of the forest who asked them why they were carrying the canoe. They said, "This canoe has served us so well and faithfully up until now, we cannot abandon it due to our sense of immense gratitude for it. Besides, we may need it again someday."

The forest dweller responded by saying, "You are now in a different landscape. Ahead of you are many miles of forest, and beyond that there are mountains so tall and majestic that they will take your breath away. Although your canoe has brought you this far, it can no longer help you make any progress on your journey. In fact, it has now become your greatest hindrance to moving forward."

When we are faced with a new set of life circumstances, and consequently experience confusion or pain, we need only let go of the way in which we are accustomed to dealing with challenges and open up to a new approach to a solution which will serve us now, here as we are.

If we ever want to know where to hear the callings of our Genius, we need look no farther than our feelings of being stuck, or our feelings of stagnation and confusion. We must realize that these feelings wouldn't even appear in our consciousness without a Genius that knows we have greater innate qualities that are not being used and that these qualities would solve many problems we currently experience. Without Genius as an inborn part of ourselves, we would simply live and be content with a stunted and brittle life because there would be no hidden gems of possibility for something greater than what we were already experiencing. We suffer because we have an unrealized destiny of something greater and more rewarding. We are dissatisfied with mediocrity and predictability because of the seeds of Genius that we carry.

I have a cat named Alvin, who, like his cartoon chipmunk namesake, is always causing some kind of trouble, like tracking fireplace ashes through the house, or occasionally using our bathtub for his litter box. He always presents us with a challenging and at times irritating situation. He is also perennially hungry. He has no talent for self-regulation when it comes to eating, so I have to monitor his food intake, lest he vomit on the carpet. He is my constant companion regardless of what I'm doing while at home, and he consistently remains within arm's length of me. Although he likes a good head scratch, his main modus operandi is to remind me to feed him. His eternal hope is that whenever I get up to do something around the house, my movement is a sign that he is going to be fed. When he feels that I have neglected him long enough, he will gently swat my face with his paw, annoyingly chew on my hair, or meow incessantly. He knows exactly how to irritate me enough to act on his behalf. His name might as well be Genius.

Here are some signs that your Genius may be calling for your attention:

- Dissatisfaction with the results of your past choices

- Relationship problems with a significant other

- Yearning for life purpose and meaning

- Psychological or physical symptoms that are hard to diagnose

- A deep urge for a career change

- Attempts to feel better by returning to premidlife behaviors that once gave pleasure or satisfaction

---

So what do we do when we realize that our underexpressed Genius is actively calling us? We will need to find ways to acknowledge and bring it into focus in our life expression, keeping in mind that expressing our Genius traits isn't necessarily accomplished by writing an award-winning symphony or creating a multimillion dollar business. Expressing Genius isn't about outward success, although success is a distinct possibility, but rather about being naturally expressive in our unique ways such as backyard projects, exploring an underdeveloped passion by returning to school, creative cooking for friends and family, or mentoring a child by helping to bring out his or her hidden genius. The essential response when Genius calls is to experiment with what is occurring to us on a deep level within our consciousness. To make this possible, we need to develop the knack of listening to ourselves in a way that we may have forgotten or never developed.

The Art of Listening

"Sometimes I go about in pity for myself,
and all the while a great wind is
bearing me across the sky."
— Ojibwa saying

The best way to frame the idea of listening for our Genius callings is to embrace the notion that while we are searching and striving for our goals, aspirations, and dreams, there is something else that wants the same for us and is calling us forward toward it. In other words, we are not alone in the struggle for self-expression and fulfillment; something else is making an effort on our behalf trying to pull us toward what we want. This something else is our guardian spirit, Genius, which already knows what will fulfill us and provide us with a rich and enjoyable life. Remember that our own unique Genius accompanied us into this life with a fully completed blueprint of what we were intended to do in order to become individual, integrated, whole people. However, most of us are completely unaware of how this pull of Genius feels or how to recognize it when it is actively calling us toward something specific.

As I write this book, my wife and I are searching for a house to buy. We have identified the parameters of what we can afford as well as the characteristics the house needs in order to provide each of us with what we value and treasure about the idea of a "home." The process of searching, seemingly endlessly, for the "just right" house is an extremely emotional one, as we mentally picture ourselves in each one, weighing the pros and cons, and trying to feel our way through the search. All the while, I've been maintaining an awareness of the fact that one of these houses is calling for us; one of these houses is the place where the next round of life lessons will take place; one of these houses wants us to be there. So while we are searching, we are also listening with as much awareness as we can summon to hear the calling of the house that is waiting for us to show up and recognize it.

The key to being able to "listen" to what is calling us toward it, or to hear the voice of our Genius, is to develop the knack of "tuning in" to our feeling selves. The feeling part of us receives signals directly from Genius in the form of images that arise simply out of nowhere. People describe some peak moments of hearing their Genius as "that moment when something in me knew that I was supposed to . . . ." Developing the knack to live in these moments, which are timeless and transcendent moments, adds the Genius dimension to our lives, and the more we take these mysterious moments of clarity seriously, the more inner guidance we can receive and use. As we develop the habit of giving credence to what is speaking to us in the quiet corner of our awareness, we can't expect anyone else to understand or agree with what we're doing. It is a solitary endeavor; we have to risk being misunderstood by others in order to understand ourselves and our Genius spirit more fully. A Sufi story illustrates this point.

Once there were four friends who travelled together frequently on spiritual pilgrimages. On one particular journey, they found themselves lost in an African desert with no food or water left. They decided to call upon God to give them an answer as to what they should do next, and they decided that they should each make individual vows to change their lives for the better in light of their precarious position.

One of the friends vowed to do more to help the poor; another made a vow to be more contemplative; the next friend committed herself to taking better care of her family. The fourth friend however, made a peculiar vow. He said simply, "I will not eat elephant meat." His three companions were upset with him. Surely this was not a vow that was worthy of God's intervention on their behalf. It seemed a convenient way for the fourth friend to remain unchanged and unrepentant. When they asked him why he had made such a strange and worthless vow, he simply said, "I don't know. It just occurred to me in the moment and it felt right."

A few hours later, as the friends were languishing in the hot desert sun, a baby elephant wandered into their camp. The first three friends saw this as a sign that God had sent them something to eat as a result of their vows to change themselves for the better. They killed and cooked the baby elephant and ate the meat. When they offered some of the life-sustaining food to the fourth friend, he declined to eat, remembering his now very inconvenient vow.

As night fell, and the four lay asleep on the sand, a huge mother elephant came charging toward them. One by one, the mother elephant smelled the breath of the first three friends, picked them up by her trunk, and smashed their bodies down on the ground. She made her way to the fourth friend, smelled his breath, picked him up with her trunk and placed him on her back. She carried him all night through the desert until morning, when she dropped him at the edge of a town, and walked away.

In our lives, we are given no guarantee that things will work out the way we want them to. But there *is* a way that things want to work out. Listening to our Genius spirit puts us on the path of this way, and when we truly see that this path is actually our own path and that we have help even in our darkest times, we can begin to trust that we are more than what we appear to be. We are larger and more expansive than we had previously thought. We are deeply connected to a mysterious source of life that moves in the depths of our awareness.

Listening Exercise

Steps to listening:

1. First, dedicate some quiet time each day to paying attention to the stirrings of your heart, where your Genius spirit resides. Whether you find your Genius by sitting in meditation or doing a centering exercise, taking a solitary walk, or reading an inspiring book. spending time paying close attention to what makes you feel a sense of openness, freedom, and excitement is the key.

2. After dedicating a special time during the day to this type of listening, choose a particular feeling that consistently arises and gives you a sense of opportunity or possibility for its expression. This feeling may come in the form of an image of some sort. Remember that an image is the most potent form of expression, appearing before thought, and containing the full expression of itself in potential. It should be an image that just makes you feel good.

3. Take the image into your conscious awareness and give it a chance to unfold. Allow it to behave like a seed in your heart, and watch as it grows and produces leaves, flowers, and fruit. What grows from tending to an image are your clues; ideas, inspirations, creative notions, and fantasies. Make sure to write down what comes to you, because this is Genius speaking and charting a course for you to take

in order to express some intrinsic and creative attribute of yourself.

4. Take an idea that you have written down and express it outwardly in whatever way occurs to you. You might pick up a guitar, open a box of paints, sit down with a pen and paper, or simply find a piece of music and begin to move your body to it. May be you'll begin to build something or to exercise. You may cook or sew. Whatever inspiration comes to you from your Genius-generated idea, follow it. Allow yourself the adventure of doing something for no reason other than responding to a wholly deep and unique part of yourself that is longing for expression.

The last point suggested in this listening exercise is particularly important to understand. You will need the courage and willingness to follow an inner impulse to express something outwardly that rarely, if ever, makes reasonable sense, especially to others. Remember that reasonableness, in terms of Genius expression, runs counter to your creative expression. There is really no such thing as creating reasonably. Creativity needs the qualities of chance, mystery, and fearlessness to be actualized and expressed. When we see Van Gogh's painting *The Starry Night*, we are not overcome with how reasonable or sensible it is. On the contrary, what moves us about the work of an artist like Van Gogh is how uniquely unreasonable and out of the box it actually is. Today, we recognize his Genius' expression, but in his lifetime, out of the over 900 paintings he created, he sold only one single painting! If he were trying to be reasonable, perhaps after the 500th painting not selling, he would have changed his style in order to suit the sensibilities of the art marketplace of the time. But he seemed to be listening to something so deeply personal and vitally important to him when he expressed himself that he literally could not have ignored it for the world.

We are all affected deeply by someone's visual representation of something taken directly from the realm of images that they have tapped into inside of themselves; someone who was following the need to express something in a way similar to a mother giving birth to a living child. Van Gogh, in this way, created an opening in his outer world for his inner world to be expressed.

We may not all paint like Van Gogh, but we all certainly possess the inner impulses to create and express in our own unique ways. We can't contrive or create these inner impulses and unique qualities, but we can allow them the space and freedom to emerge. Our effort to give them a chance to come to the surface brings the deep sense of satisfaction that we are seeking. We find fulfillment from participating with our Genius spirit, making time and space in our lives for its qualities to be expressed.

A Redefinition of Midlife

One salient feature of our psychology in midlife is the realization that our lives aren't going to last forever. We begin to notice new physical aches and pains, our hair slowly beginning to grey or disappear, and looking in the mirror and seeing an older person that we don't quite recognize is a daily surprise. Even though, somehow, we always knew this time would come, at some point, we are confronted with the eventuality of our own physical death. When a thought starts to come to us weekly or even daily, it's a sure sign that something deep in our psyche is giving us a nudge or a poke to take a serious look at the message it is sending. Thoughts of our eventual death need not be seen as morbidity. They can also be encountered with our curious and creative nature as a call for introspection and action.

I remember reading an article in the LA Weekly in the late 1980s by Michael Ventura entitled "You in Particular Are Going to Die." Even though I was not in midlife at the time, the article spoke to me about the personal responsibility that each of us carries for living our lives with the knowledge that they are finite and therefore precious. I felt the need to carry the idea, on some level, that one way or another, at some undetermined time, my life as I know it will end. This realization casts a unique and sobering light on our situation as human beings, and is particularly useful at midlife as a wake up call to stop postponing things that we have always wanted to do. We cannot wait any longer to embody the qualities of character that we have always wanted to show to the world.

If aging is known to be a universal human experience that happens gradually over time, why do so many of us experience a certain pivotal moment when the realization of our own aging comes as such a terrible shock? Although we all have different temporal demarcations in our personal timelines of our lives as to when and where midlife and aging actually occur, the proverbial midlife cat is out of the bag usually between the ages of 35 and 50. Through advances in medicine, cosmetic surgery, and a wealth of information on practicing healthier lifestyles, we may be able to prolong the idea of our physical youth, but the day eventually comes when there is no denying that we have crossed the threshold into midlife. Some of us confront this passage kicking and screaming, while others may simply waltz right over the line with grace and acceptance. On the midlife side of the door, the world appears differently, because we are seeing our lives in terms of how much time we have left as opposed to how much time we have already lived. This shift in focus, this view from the hill of midlife requires a redefinition of our life story that includes our learned experiences as well as a new, more useful orientation aimed at where we are going with the rest of our lives. Through living this long, we can see things through the lens of experience that were not visible before, and this helps to shape the new path we decide to take.

Whatever images of midlife we had held before will need to be amended once we have arrived and it has become a reality. In order to thrive in this new reality and move forward, we will need to reimagine our lives from exactly where we currently find ourselves.

Re-Imagining Midlife

There are few things more difficult and painful than trying to live our current lives through the images we had created for ourselves in a different stage of life. We may not remember creating ourselves in a previous stage, but nonetheless, day by day, we developed a sense of self through experiencing life's varied colors and qualities and living with the consequences of the choices we've made along the way. If we want a fruitful and interesting midlife, we need to move forward and continue to grow, which requires us to develop the knack of letting go of many of the ideas about ourselves we've accepted up until now. These old ideas have become psychological hindrances, and actively moving away from them through conscious effort gives us an unexpected source of inner strength that is sorely needed on the journey.

Midlife Growth

Growth is not a word that is commonly used to describe what occurs at midlife. Usually the word *crisis* appears next to the word *midlife*, and this crisis is commonly seen as a midlife *inevitability*, heralding a type of decline in our expansion as human beings. We are expected to buy a red convertible, take on a younger partner, cut or dye our hair, but we eventually see that these outward things don't work while we give up and watch our vitality slip away. A common belief is that expansiveness is characteristic of youth, identity is formed by midlife, and that we ride that same identity into old age. Far from this being true, midlife is when we actually need an identity change or modification in order to continue to deepen as individuals.

We can see growth and development in its many forms taking place in childhood. These changes happen so automatically that the advent of growth is something that is taken for granted. It is assumed that children will grow physically and psychologically. In early adulthood, however, growth is not as obvious. Physical growth has stopped, and our individual psychologies have formed enough to orient us in the navigation of our worlds. Growth mostly occurs in spite of us, mostly through the necessity of accepting and overcoming the inevitabilities and limitations that are part of our daily life experience. At midlife, another opportunity is afforded us, and that is to take conscious responsibility for the time we have left, thereby turning the remaining portion of our lives into a new kind of growth process. This process is fueled by the turning of our awareness inward to our individualism and then responding outwardly with its unique expression. We begin to live deliberately and purposefully by using the experiences we have already lived through as ballast to steady our ship for the journey into our futures.

Midlife is actually a time to exercise one of our greatest and undervalued innate qualities: the imagination. The first thing to realize is that it's okay to imagine great things for ourselves. Why not? All creative experience and expression begins by imagining something that doesn't yet exist. I'm not talking about a program where we imagine our dreams and desires into existence or about manifesting our desires by creating dream boards with images of material possessions and lifestyles from magazine cutouts. The kind of reimagining needed at midlife has to do with an inner identity that better reflects who we are and who we would like to be going forward. This type of imagining is an inner movement toward aligning ourselves with the Genius qualities and traits in us that may have lain dormant up until now. When we are allied with our own innate qualities, we may or may not see new possessions appearing and things working out differently in our outer lives, but these are peripheral events compared to what we're truly trying to bring about. At midlife, uncovering a sense of purpose and meaning is on the top of the list of priorities for most of us, having seen that merely possessing something or creating the perfect circumstances on the outside doesn't and cannot deepen our life experience.

Engaging in deliberate creative imagination is a synthesis of being both childlike and wise. Wisdom is gained through experience, and experience ultimately acknowledges the importance of seeing things from a state of innocence. This innocence is not ignorance; it is not the lack of knowing things, but a knowledgeable and deliberate reintegration with our Genius's unstoppable creativity and unlimited potential. Our human potential is always realized by first embracing what seems to be a fantasy of what could be.

A New Definition of Perfection

As we search for the perfect life, we are usually identifying perfection as the absence of conflict and the achievement of the correct circumstances, such as

- an adequate or surplus supply of money
- a fulfilling career
- a loving relationship
- optimum physical health
- a comfortable home
- the recognition and respect of others

If we can merely observe our lives impersonally over time, we will discover that regardless of how close we have come to these idealistic circumstances, we see them as mostly achieved by others; we see them as enviable possibilities that we haven't been able to create for ourselves — at least not permanently. Our idea of perfection relies mainly on comparing ourselves to others, based on our view from outside their lives and our projections onto them. From this false perception of the lives and circumstances of others, we may live with a sense of shame and feelings of inadequacy for not having arrived at the perfect place.

What is needed desperately by those of us who want lives of happiness and fulfillment is a new definition of perfection that takes into consideration the whole of our human experience as a great life experiment.

Long before we learned to compare ourselves to others as a way of gauging perfection and success, in our early childhood, it was enough for us just to be as we were. We were perfect. We laughed, cried, and played. We fought with our siblings, we made up. We got sick and then healed. We got punished and then forgiven. All of life's possibilities were open to us to explore without the responsibility of forcing any kind of outcome, and we didn't judge anything as failures or successes. All of our experiences were a process of deepening our character and of becoming unique individuals who were finding their place in the world.

As we grew and became more integrated into our societies, the natural feeling of individual worth eventually gave way to an idea of perfection that we needed to achieve in order to please our parents, teachers, and friends. We succumbed to the idea that there was a whole world out there of which we knew nothing and were completely unprepared to navigate. As we scrambled to catch up with everyone else, we forgot that we were once perfect just as we were, with our naïveté, our skinned knees, our fantasies, and our disappointments.

We are called at midlife finally to embrace a mature model of perfection that transcends our adolescent reactionary one. We will need to redefine for ourselves, through our gained experience and wisdom, a vision of human life that contains the polarities of joy and suffering, gain and loss, love and heartbreak, and health and illness as components of a perfect life. These experiences happen to everyone to some extent, and if we want to call them imperfect, then we're taking exception to the ways of the universe itself. We are actually saying that existence, which provides these experiences to each individual, is somehow wrong and needs to be fixed.

The perfect life indeed contains the polarities of experience as well as a good deal of conflict and difficulty. If we can acknowledge that we actually need these things to grow and develop as authentic individuals, we can see that their absence is what would make our lives imperfect. Without them, we would have no way to challenge outdated beliefs, overcome perceived limitations, or expand our awareness of ourselves. In fact, we can thank the difficulties that we strenuously avoid for the potential growth that they can provide us. There is no amount of easy, outward success that can deepen us as much as encountering and overcoming difficulties can.

So, in redefining the perfect life during midlife, using the life lessons we've collected as valuable information, we can include every experience that arrives at our door going forward as part of *the perfection of life* instead of our perfect life. We will see that it is far better to move with what existence is sending us as perfect rather than to attempt to contrive perfection out of a limited and fearful mindset. As we open ourselves to the larger possibilities of personal fulfillment and purpose, we will include our bumps and scrapes as well as our hugs and kisses as the perfection of a more expansive life experience.

Letting Go to Move Forward

In order to embrace the intention to let our Genius qualities manifest in our lives, we will need to correct an outdated concept that may have helped us thus far in life but that no longer serves us in our current situation. As already concluded, the main way to move toward uncovering the innate talents and qualities of our Genius is by developing the knack of letting go of what no longer works. I love the word *knack*. It implies more of a felt intuition being used rather than depending on something that can be taught. It carries a poetic quality, much like the language spoken by our Genius. Developing the proficiency or knack of letting go is ripened by our excursions into the sometimes dim and moonlit world of our dreams and fantasies. We will need to be willing to let our consciousness flow like water into places inside of us that many people won't let themselves go. For many of us, especially in the West, that idea is a frightening one: If we let go, then what's to stop our world from falling apart? Wouldn't that be irresponsible of us? What about our obligations to our families and communities?

If we explore our fears a little more closely, we will discover that at midlife, we may be running on the fumes of an empty fuel tank. Still, we try to give and be responsible in the old way, and, of course, this is a drain on our available energy. Midlife is a time for refueling, a process that may take the shape of something that looks selfish to others. This is the time to take care of ourselves in a way that promotes our creativity and vitality, which in turn can be given to others. The saying "I can only spend what is in my own pocket" applies here. The real responsibility in midlife is therefore to make sure we actually have something in our pocket before we try and give to others. Luckily, a secret pocket we have yet to discover is filled with our inexhaustible Genius. The energy that comes from living and expressing it doesn't come from a limited energy source, but from a part of us whose nature is fullness.

Many centuries ago, a Chinese wise man named Lao Tsu was about to leave his village because he was tired of living with shallow people who were unable to comprehend life in a state of letting go. On his way out of the village, Lao Tsu was stopped by the village gatekeeper, who refused to let him leave until he had written down his teachings for posterity. Lao Tsu was reluctant, but he finally relented and wrote 81 verses about how to live life in the *Tao*, or the *way of the universe*. The first sentence he wrote was revealing: "The Tao that can be named is not the eternal Tao." He is indicating here that an explanation or description of the Tao is no more the actual thing than a recipe for chocolate cake is a chocolate cake. In order to derive some benefit from the Tao, one has to experience or be it. So it is with Genius. It is not enough to describe it, although it is a tempting distraction; we need to find it in our marrow, where it actually resides, and be brave (or desperate) enough to let it out as our unique expression into the world.

Nature itself in midlife makes us ready to look into ourselves and to live our Genius by the gradual removal of many aspects of our younger selves. Besides noticing unfamiliar aches and pains in our bodies, we can see a loss of elasticity of our skin. Things that were once strong and firm begin to give way to the force of gravity; things move downward as if to say: "It's time to get grounded and find your center." With the advent of aging, therefore, when less time and energy is spent trying to appear a certain way or to hold on to an old identity, more and more we find ourselves freed up to pay attention to our inner world where our Genius is alive and well and eternally youthful.

The Knacks

In order to take full advantage of our experiences while uncovering our Genius qualities, it is necessary to develop several "knacks" that will aid in the endeavor of living the rest of our lives as insightful and dynamic individuals. Knacks are defined here as natural or learned skills of performing a task. Knacks can carry the essence of wisdom and mastery. They are the tools of an awake and aware person who has learned something and is practicing and perfecting what he or she has learned. Knacks become our second nature when we practice them.

The term *second nature* comes from the Latin phrase *secundum naturam,* meaning "according to nature" or "following nature." It is taken to mean that if we respond to a situation consistently, we acquire the tendency to act from our inner character or instinct effortlessly whenever we are presented with the same situation. To acquire these second nature tendencies, we must be presented with a situation over and over again in order to practice. Luckily, life is incredibly generous in providing challenging situations for us to hone our second nature tendencies or knacks.

The knacks that we will need to develop for the purpose of finding our Genius qualities at midlife are these:

- Forgiving ourselves and others
- Seeing failures as valuable experiences
- Acknowledging our successes
- Moving with what is flowing or happening in the present moment

If we see ourselves as the helmsman of our ship, our job isn't to control the wind, rain, or tides but rather to respond to these naturally occurring elements with our talent for correcting the course of our vessel. We have the goal of Genius expression as our heading, and if the wind blows from the south, we adjust our sails accordingly to keep our ship pointed in the right direction. If the waves become large and choppy, we may lower the sails temporarily to ride out the storm. If we drift too close to land, we may wait for the tides to rise again to set sail. Whatever elements life throws our way, our knack of responding to them creatively and expressively becomes our second nature and will keep us moving toward our goal and destination.

Confucius at the Cataract

It is said that once, Confucius and some of his students were walking by a large waterfall that fell with such force and volume that it created a gigantic whirlpool in the river below it. Such was the intensity of the whirling water that anything that came near it would be pulled into its trap. They noticed that an old man was standing at the top of the waterfall and, all at once, jumped straight into the whirlpool! Confucius was alarmed at the sight of someone apparently committing suicide, so they all ran down to the rivers edge to see if there was anything they could do to save the man.

Just as they arrived at the mighty whirlpool, they saw the old man pop up in the calm part of the river, merrily swimming around, enjoying himself. Confucius said to the man, "I thought you were a spirit, but now I see that you are a man. How do you manage this amazing feat that we just witnessed?" to which the old man answered, "It's simple, really – I merely jump into the whirl and come out with the swirl. I accommodate myself to the water, and not the water to me. By not forcing my will on the situation, the whirlpool spits me out at the bottom, and I simply rise back to the top in calm water. I have been doing this since I was a little boy, and so the practice of it has become second nature to me."

The story of the old man demonstrates that the key to developing the knacks that will help us to allow our Genius talents to emerge comes from the practice of *responding* to our challenges instead of *reacting* to them. A reaction will always contain an element of force in our basic resistance to whatever experience is coming our way. Conversely, a response allows us to accommodate ourselves to the immediate situation without fighting; we simply go in with the whirl and come out with the swirl. This is one of the most important things we can actualize at midlife: the Genius quality of working with what is presented to us instead of forcing our will upon the world. Genius doesn't need to struggle to express itself. It is already 100 percent complete. We just need to catch up with it and allow it its proper place in our lives.

Forgiveness

One of the most undervalued knacks is the capacity for forgiveness. This knack, in order to be the most beneficial to us in our quest for midlife growth, must be exercised and applied to both ourselves and others. Many of us are able to forgive others' transgressions against us but are unable to forgive our own. Others among us can forgive our own shortcomings but cannot let go of the grudge we carry against someone else. Forgiveness, however, is the only way forward. The act of forgiveness doesn't condone the offences committed against ourselves or against others, but it allows us the freedom to move past our fixations on hurting and having been hurt. With the vision afforded to us by living as long as midlife, we can act with compassion for ourselves and others by seeing the mistakes we have made and endeavoring not to make them again. Forgiveness makes us rich by giving us back our inner mobility concerning the places we have been stuck. It allows us to flow once more beyond the emotional boulders that have blocked our way for far too long. Forgiveness allows us to remember the import of the lesson without eternally reenacting the offences over and over again in our consciousness. It can release us from a self-imposed prison we have created that promises to keep us safe from bad things ever happening again but actually dooms us to an unending, hellish repetition of the very things that we're trying to resolve and finally put to rest.

Failure as Inspiration

We all fail. Failure is as much a part of every human life as breathing and eating. But dwelling on our failures is missing the point of them. Failures are simply dead ends that we have encountered, either by experimentation or heedlessness. The experience of failure can be a rich and fertile source of information about what not to do or where not to go. Failure can be seen as a way of ruling out something for good, giving us the freedom to look elsewhere for a solution.

Failure, seen through a creative Genius lens, is actually the harbinger of new beginnings and directions. I am not prescribing a simple attitude of positivity but rather an acknowledgment of an actual dynamic of the creative process. Seeing the entirety of our life as our greatest piece of art, we are not afraid to fail along the way as we experiment with different colors and textures in order to get it right. Our eventual success is all the more rich and valuable specifically because of the failures we have encountered on the journey. Failure is not the opposite of success; it is the fertile ground that nourishes, supports, and sustains it. As we endeavor in the great art project of our personal individuation, what we learn as a result of failure comprises the deep and enormous body of the iceberg, and success is the small tip that is visible above the surface. It feels great to see the tip representing success risen above the

> "Negative results are just what I want. They're just as valuable to me as positive results. I can never find the thing that does the job best until I find the ones that don't."
> —*Thomas A. Edison*

water with the glint of sunlight on it, but it is equally important to acknowledge the great mass of lived experience below, supporting and stabilizing it.

Acknowledging Daily Successes

Another knack that applies to our wealth of experience is the ability to acknowledge our successes, large and small. Many of us have a difficult time with this because we have learned that to dwell on our accomplishments is somehow narcissistic and selfish. We have been told that it is for others to recognize and congratulate us on our successes. It is impossible however for others to know the small victories we attain, such as the daily breaking of a habit, forgiving ourselves for something done or left undone, and having a good day in spite of difficulties and challenges. Acknowledging successes large and small means that we are paying attention; we are shining an inner light on the things that take place in order to amplify and deepen our knowledge of ourselves as people who succeed daily at things. Instead of dwelling on how we consistently fall short of the ideal of what we "should" be, our focus can be on what is actually happening with us, feet on the ground, head in the game. We can and must give ourselves the permission to be a success. Whatever the level of the success, acknowledging it can change the way in which we move through our lives. With the acknowledgement of this success, we are using part of our wealth of experience as much needed fuel for our journey.

Flowing with the present

Perhaps the most important knack of all is the ability to keep moving in spite of the obstacles we may find on our path as we live from day to day. It takes the wisdom that comes from years and years of lived experience to be able to summon the agility of consciousness needed to follow the flow of life as it is presented to us in the moment. This wisdom tells us that even though we may be facing a dilemma that seems quite impossible to overcome, we have already lived through similar or even worse situations that have come and gone again and again. At midlife, we already know the pain of having tried to resist the changes in our lives that have taken place, and we finally have enough perspective from the first half of our life to know that the changes happen whether we resist or not. Now, we have earned the capacity to choose to accept what the present moment is bringing us as a gift for our further development as deeper and more nuanced human beings. Flowing with the present moment is a poetic response to the mysterious universal intelligence that is choreographing this world-play that we find ourselves in. It is a creative response that can enliven and invigorate us by having to step outside of the entrenched routines we have created for ourselves. The fact is, we need daily challenges and difficulties in order to continue to truly be alive. And a quality of the universe is to provide them to us in whatever guise necessary in order to accomplish this goal.

Stop It

Comedian Bob Newhart, in his TV role as a psychiatrist, presented a hilarious skit involving a client coming to him with her fear of being buried alive. His advice to her was simply to "stop it!" This seems like terrible advice and treatment from a trained professional—so simplistic and noninsightful. But there is wisdom in its simplicity. If we go past the laugh value of the advice, we can actually find a kernel of truth here.

As a psychotherapist, I would rarely recommend that one of my clients simply "stop it" when he or she had come to me for help. I realize that there is always a compelling reason for why people feel as they do and why certain fears play a large role in their life experience. Part of my work and approach is to honor fears, defenses, and symptoms and give them their proper place in my clients' life expressions. I have found that acknowledging these things as serving a vital importance in the overall functioning of the psyche is the fastest and most effective way to integrate and lessen their impact on daily functioning. Certainly, my advice to those reading this book is to seek out professional therapeutic help with any persistent fears or symptoms that keep them from living their lives as they would like to live them.

Having made my case, there can also come a time when the advice to "stop it" has immense value. Most of us by midlife have developed simply by having lived a certain number of years performing a series of physical, mental, and emotional habits that are now repeating automatically. We're driving in a car, but we are no longer behind the wheel; our habits are driving us, and we're passed out drunk in the back seat. The knack that is needed here is to begin to make the attempt to take the wheel back from our habits. Regardless of how much therapy we receive, there comes a time when we literally will need to stop engaging in habits that no longer serve us in taking us where we want to go.

The wonderful thing about this time of "stopping it" is that it, by definition, brings us into the present moment, the tiniest container of time, where we can actually stop a habit by forgiving ourselves or others; acknowledge our successes, large and small; and see our failures as signposts instead of tombstones. The present moment is literally the only place where we can actually put down the fourth slice of pizza, allow our hearts to forgive, smile at something that has gone our way, and change direction when we hit a wall. "Stopping it" means to move deliberately into new, uncharted territory where we have literally unlimited potential for change and growth. The more we can make small changes in our habits, the less burdened with the past we become. If anything is needed on a midlife journey, it is the lightness that comes from unburdening ourselves of things that no longer serve us: failures, regrets, perceived limitations, and above all, habits that keep us frozen in our past.

We can see that, in a way, our physical existence actually depends on "stopping it." Every time we breathe in, we immediately need to "stop it" and breathe out. We can't insist that we only inhale out of the fear that if we exhale, no more breath will come. We obviously have a deep, implicit trust that our breath will continue to come into and move out of our lungs; we must trust our breathing in order to function on even a basic level. We will need to take this quality of trust into the more conscious realm of experience, where we learn to trust that our lives are carried by the same intelligence that moves our breath. We can then allow things that no longer serve a purpose to go, while we allow the things that support the continuation of our midlife journey to come to us in the new space we have created by letting go of them.

Ambition vs. Purpose

In our adolescence and young adulthood, it was necessary to listen to the drives of ambition and respond to the need to accomplish things that would help us to define ourselves. During that period, we had a genuine need to build our identities into something "solid" to give ourselves the illusion of permanency in order to exist as a separate, egoic entity. These drives, although necessary, also serve the purpose of taking us so far away from our natural selves and our Genius traits that, by midlife, a course correction is desperately needed. Again, our friend Lao Tsu says,

> I do not know its name.
> Call it Tao.
> For lack of a better word, I call it great.
> Being great, it flows.
> It flows far away.
> Having gone far, it returns.
> Returning is the motion of the Tao.

Midlife brings a longing to return to our roots. Old memories and ways of expression and creativity begin to surface in our consciousness, calling us to revisit the organic parts of ourselves that we left behind in order to chase our ambitions, which embody our ideas about what we needed to be happy. Ambition can take us only so far before we realize the emptiness of its nature and its inability ultimately to satisfy us. Ambition is the shadow of purpose. It stands in as its substitute during the first half of life. Midlife carries an innate urgency for meaning and purpose, and purpose is always found by hanging around with our Genius.

In adolescence and young adulthood, it stands to reason that we emulate others' behaviors and habits as a way of creating identity. Not being absorbed in our Genius qualities, we can't see a better way. But by midlife, if we are listening carefully to our symptoms, we can trace our discomfort back to an inauthentic expression of ourselves that stems from "borrowing" others' ideas and ideals. This discomfort is actually our Genius's way of getting our attention. Its message is that our life's meaning and purpose has already been written on the walls of our souls; we need only to return consciously to that realm in order to embrace it and bring it out into the world.

Why do we need to express our Genius outwardly? One undeniable fact is that we are human, with a physical body in a physical world. We are only here for an unknowable, finite amount of time. Many seekers of enlightenment choose to deny the body and the human experience, dismissing them as "distractions" from a transcendent existence. But we have to ask ourselves: If there is such a thing as meaning and purpose in human existence, would it be life denying? Wouldn't it include life in all of its aspects including the physical world? What makes the physical world and all of its aspects less "spiritual" than the rest of creation?

The Hindu and Buddhist traditions have a word for illusion: *maya*. Many people take on the idea that "the world is maya" and is therefore a distraction from ultimate reality.

But what if the idea of *maya* is seen poetically, meaning that it's not that the world is illusion but that *the way we see the world is illusory*. It follows that what is needed is not a denial of the world but a change in our vision to a way of perceiving the world more authentically.

From the outlook of Genius, we are able to see the physical world as it is, and as a natural consequence, we can see our place in it. Genius, with its gift-giving nature, is simply acting naturally by outwardly expressing itself. As we allow it space in our lives, it gives of itself in a myriad of creative expressions and magically brings us a sense of personal fulfillment. *Ambition* can thus be seen as an imposition of ourselves onto the world, whereas *purpose* is our Genius contributing to the world. Ambition wants to conquer; purpose wants to share.

3

Living the Essential

Most of us, with few exceptions, have abandoned at least some of the expressions of our Genius spirit long ago in childhood. Of course, at the time, we didn't realize that for the sake of practicality and the necessity of building a healthy ego with which to integrate with our society, we were also closing off an essential part of ourselves in the process. Note that I'm using the word *essential* here, from the Latin *essentia*, meaning "being, essence." Calling something *essential* or *elemental* indicates that without it, we are not complete or are missing something central to our true identity. When we have lost something so important, as in the case of Genius, a basic function of our psyche is activated, namely, the effort to return to a state of energetic balance. This function calls to us and creates opportunities in the outer world for us to experience and thereby reclaim that essential thing that has been lost. Many times the opportunities created for us by this deeper part of ourselves seem irrelevant to the purpose for which they were intended. But if we take a step back and view some of our past experiences from a Genius perspective, we can see our basic need for psychic and existential balance and wholeness at play, mysteriously weaving opportunities into our lives for us to gain insight, strength, and wisdom.

Midlife and *The Little Prince*

In the classic book, *The Little Prince*, by Antoine de St. Exupery, we can see an example of how these life experiences can occur and how random and bizarre they may appear to us at the time. The narrator of the story is a pilot going through a midlife transformation, who encounters the Little Prince. This boy, an alien child who has fallen to Earth from a tiny asteroid, can be seen as the pilot's Genius spirit that he came upon by "accident" at a particularly challenging life-or-death situation in his life. We can use this story to illustrate and lay out a framework of the transformation at midlife that can come from encountering and integrating your Genius into your life. It's interesting to note that although St. Exupery was in fact a real-life pilot, he didn't give the pilot in the story a name, which can indicate that this is everyone's story and that everyone is given opportunities to encounter something mysterious and yet distantly familiar to us. Our role in this exchange is to follow the clues the experience provides and to be available to incorporate the inevitable changes they will bring to our conscious lives.

The story begins when the plane our Pilot is flying over the Sahara desert breaks down, forcing him to land 1000 miles from any human habitation. He is painfully aware that if he can't fix his plane himself, he will certainly die there, isolated and alone. At midlife, many of us are similarly confronted with a life that just isn't working anymore. We may have a family, pay the bills, go to work, but life has generally lost any color or flavor. We're living in an empty desert, devoid of meaning and life purpose. Many question if life is even worth living in this place, and our focus turns from thinking about how long we have lived to wondering how much time we have left to live. The introduction of the reality of eventual death brings a certain urgency to midlife. We begin to ponder existential questions that had not been a part of our thought process before, and we often feel that part of us has already died. But the part that lives on through the passing of our physical youth yearns for something that will bring meaning and purpose to our lives. It is at this desperate point that our little prince, our Genius, can be encountered again, and we can revisit our natural qualities and talents abandoned in our youth in order to breathe fresh life into our current existence.

Our pilot falls asleep on the sand and, in the morning, is awakened by a strange little voice that asks him to draw a sheep. The pilot is shocked and confused as to how a small boy has arrived at the exact place where he had broken down, in the middle of nowhere. But without any explanation, the little prince insists on the pilot drawing him a sheep. Faced with this inexplicable mystery, the pilot decides to try:

> When a mystery is too overpowering, one dare not disobey. Absurd as it might seem to me, a thousand miles from any human habitation and in danger of death, I took out of my pocket a sheet of paper and my fountain-pen. But then I remembered how my studies had been concentrated on geography, history, arithmetic and grammar, and I told the little chap (a little crossly, too) that I did not know how to draw. He answered me: "That doesn't matter. Draw me a sheep."

Having a breakdown of the confidence we had lived with during the first half of our lives is not necessarily a bad thing. Sometimes in order to correct our course, we have to shut down the engines that had only taken us in one direction. We need fresh energy in order to change course, because the previous internal drives don't work anymore. We can find that energy in the eternal qualities of our Genius, which was there in us at birth and which continues to exist just as potently at midlife.

Due to our habit of largely ignoring our Genius, the things that it asks of us when we begin to listen again to its voice may seem confusing and mysterious. We may feel the urge to paint, though we never had learned to paint, we may come up with an idea for a book, or we may feel the need to travel to a place we've always wanted to visit. Remember that these urges may seem foolish or silly to others in our lives and may appear as odd and strange even to ourselves. Explorations of any kind have often been seen as fools' errands to those who stay behind, never daring to leave the familiar for the unknown. As a psychotherapist, I have often helped my clients differentiate feelings of fear from those of excitement. In the misinterpretation of these two feelings, we could sacrifice an adventure that would greatly enrich us. Excitement about the prospect of encountering a new view from a vista, for instance, might be confused with the fear of falling off a cliff. The fear of the explorer, however, turns into excitement about something new that requires the resources of our original, innate Genius. Even though we may not know how to do what the Genius is asking, owing to the fact that we've ignored its calling until now, it doesn't matter. At midlife, it is better to be a struggling but happy dancer than a miserable yet successful businessperson. The need for change is so great that we begin to listen to our Genius and honor its requests, even when unaware of how that could possibly help our situation.

After many attempts at drawing a sheep for the Little Prince, and all of them rejected, the pilot does something unexpected, even to himself. He draws a box with air holes on the side and explains that the sheep is inside the box. This pleases the Little Prince so much because he is able to look inside the box to see the sheep inside, asleep. The pilot recalls, *"My friend never explained anything to me. He thought, perhaps, that I was like himself. But I, alas, do not know how to see sheep through the walls of boxes. Perhaps I am a little like the grown-ups. I have had to grow old."*

Upon hearing the callings of our Genius again, we, like the pilot, may become sadly aware of how we have become old in our thinking and in our view of ourselves and the universe. Even though the pilot began drawing as a child, he was discouraged from doing so by the "grown ups" in his life, and so he gave up his drawing career in exchange for a more practical one. We may not have taken the time in our adulthood to engage in creative activity simply for the pleasure of it. So we shouldn't be surprised when trying on our Genius shoes once again that we've become a little bit rusty at living our childhood dreams. Nonetheless, we can do something unexpected. Getting in touch with our Genius talents can allow us to act "outside the box" and express something in a unique and authentic way. Albert Einstein famously stated, " We cannot solve our problems with the same thinking we used when we created them." Like the box drawn for the sheep, allowing ourselves to express our Genius solves a problem that no amount of our old way of thinking can solve. The mysterious opportunities and challenges presented to us can push us in a direction toward which we would normally never go in order to come up with a creative solution. The fact is, we won't be able to navigate through midlife's terrain with the same vehicle we've used in early adulthood. We will need a new mode of transportation that uses our untapped Genius as a source of energy. So it is highly advantageous for us to be on the lookout for our Little Prince/Genius as we move about in our lives. The opportunities it presents are unique and essential to our reemergence as creatively living individuals who have at their center a guiding spirit that can lead us to what is specifically fulfilling and meaningful for us.

Genius and Reeducation

One of the steps needed to uncover our Genius at midlife can be explained by exploring some traditional ways in which Genius was detected and encouraged in individual at a time when education included the awareness of the Genius spirit.

In our contemporary society, we have an education system that is focused on learning through the introduction and study of written materials and the practicing of skills and techniques specific to a certain field that have proven to be effective. All of this knowledge is to be imported from the outside world into our intellectual and technical understanding, and the purpose of studying this information is to create an informed and "educated" person. The more students can grasp the idea of the material being presented to them and can, in turn, prove their understanding through reexplanation and demonstration of the ideas or techniques, the more educated they are said to be.

But what if our current idea of education has a dimension that is being completely overlooked? What if an education actually originally included guiding students to become richer and more fulfilled people inwardly as well? Most schools' and universities' curriculums don't include the notion that studying and understanding certain areas of knowledge will make us fuller, deeper, and more satisfied people. Rewarding self-growth through education has for the most part been lost to us.

The word *education* can be traced from the Latin word *educere,* which means "to bring forth." Working with the idea of a Genius spirit in each individual, an education was originally meant to help bring out one's Genius so that its unique qualities would become a blueprint for one's learning and life expression. Instead of only supplying outer knowledge and instruction, teachers, would help students uncover their inbuilt Genius traits. Doing so would point out and indicate their strengths and talents for expressing their particular colors and flavors in their chosen field. Because of the uniqueness of each person, each one's individual perspective and expression of those strengths and talents would be one of a kind and could never be repeated by anyone else in any authentic way.

Because there is and will be literally only one of each of us, it is uniquely important to "bring forth" our Genius and allow its expression to manifest in the world. We can see this expression as no less than an existential mandate, since existence has gone to the trouble to imbue us with our inner Genius qualities for the purpose of outward expression. Although it may sound like a bit like hubris, it can be argued that we are literally depriving the world (or the part of the world we have the opportunity to touch) of the Genius gifts we have come here to give. In the light of this truth, being a little hubristic can be a good and even necessary thing.

In his book, *The Icarus Deception*, author Seth Godin speaks about the well-known Greek myth of Icarus, who, against his father Daedalus' warnings to not fly too close to the sun, became so enamored with his God-like powers to fly, did fly too close, melted the wax which held his wings together, and plummeted to his death into the sea. Icarus' heedlessness of Daedalus' warning not to fly too high has been used as an example of the hubris of youth and its dire consequences. This mythic event has served as a lesson for lowering the expectations of one's creative potential for the sake of not crashing and burning if one fails. But in this myth, as Godin points out, the second and generally unknown piece of advise to Icarus was to not fly too close to the sea. In other words, Icarus, don't fly too low either. Don't expect too little of yourself. This further advice indicates that we shouldn't sell ourselves too short or take an apologetic stance when it comes to expressing our creativity, lest the water keep our wings from being able to rise with the wind as they could and should. It is therefore not hubris but instead part of the creative human spirit to reach for greater and more rewarding forms of self-expression that stem from our Genius qualities.

If we don't succumb to the falsehood of our uniqueness making us better than others, we can be fully engaged in the great pleasure of being our one-of-a-kind selves. Just as each single sunflower, being similar yet unique in its form, stands alongside others like itself, together creating a magnificent field of yellow, we as human flowers can live and express ourselves alongside each other without fear of losing our individuality. Our Genius qualities are never competitive with others' Genius qualities; they are meant to compliment and inspire each other. Competition comes from the need to be better than another because of a fear of being less than and, ultimately, valueless. This fear simply comes from the insecurity of not knowing the value of our innate Genius qualities, because our Genius has not been brought out, discovered, honored, and explored. When our Genius spirit is given expression, we experience a state of creative fearlessness accompanied by a sense of deep satisfaction. We are fully engaged in our life's work and therefore have no time to dwell in comparison or competition.

Because of the basic, inbuilt need of our Genius to be expressive, we are beset with the urge and the urgency to uncover our own channels for the giving of our Genius gifts. At midlife, it becomes clear to many of us that we have not been properly educated in the ways of our Genius spirit. It's qualities and properties weren't properly brought forth, acknowledged, or encouraged by our parents or teachers. For most of us, if we've found any qualities of Genius at all, it has been on our own and largely in spite of others' lack of encouragement. Many of us have had to suffer to express something completely natural in ourselves. We may also have received the message through others' lack of support and incomprehension that by focusing our attention and effort on this creative expression, we were being selfish and indulgent. If so, instead of feeling deep satisfaction from the discovery and expression of Genius, the experience is tinged with a sense of suffering, making it a bittersweet, somewhat lonely experience. For many of us, it is time to reeducate ourselves by leading our Genius out of hiding with a sense of purpose, responsibility, and gratitude.

In order to facilitate our education in the qualities our Genius wants to express, we have to look to our childhood. Finding a time before we had accepted others' ideas and plans for us and before we unknowingly borrowed a more limited and artificial version of who we are is the key to rediscovering our initial, innocent dreams and yearnings. These aspirations are still present and available to us if we sincerely look for them. At midlife, since we can't unknow what we now know from many years of life experience, we will see and remember our childhood experiences differently when we look back and try to revive something that was important to us. This is actually a good thing, because we now have the ability, in light of our many successes and failures, to see the value in the authentic expression of ourselves. By now, we have made the effort to live the *idea* of the person we were supposed to be, only to find that it doesn't really work. We can see that in order to live as an authentic person, initially, we need to return to our genuine and innate interests that we had as children. From there, we can find the clues necessary to uncover Genius in our present life.

As children, we have no choice but to assume that our parents and other grownups know more than we do about the world. Out of necessity, children trust the grownups in their lives to guide them, because they have no life experience to call upon. This trust almost invariably is broken when an authority figure fails to recognize and encourage the individuality in a child. The child then automatically adopts the ideals, conditions, and concepts of the adult, regardless of them having little to do with the child's innate qualities. Most of us are therefore engaged in living a disingenuous life from an early age, and only at a certain stage of life do we recognize that something is sorely missing from our life experience. We're feeling the effects of the long-time disregard of our Genius qualities, and the lack of acknowledgement of and connection to this guiding spirit has manifested in symptoms of dissatisfaction and lack of enthusiasm for what we have been doing up until now. Luckily, Genius doesn't go away regardless of how long we've ignored it. It is so much an intrinsic part of us that it speaks to us constantly, using the language of image, symbol, and dreams in order to make its presence known to us. Regardless of how far from it we've gone, the fact that we can feel that something is missing from our lives is the proof that Genius is speaking through symptom and emotion.

Relocating the innocent spark from our childhood that organically wanted to express itself may not be an easy task. Some of us remember exactly our spark of Genius, and some of us may have buried it (for many good reasons) deeply in our unconscious. But regardless of our particular situation concerning the original Genius impulses, there are always breadcrumbs left by the Genius on whatever path we took when we unknowingly left it behind.

Leading out our Genius or educating ourselves on what it wants to express necessarily takes us into the realm of dreams, imagination, and fantasy. Many of us have been taught that this realm has absolutely no substantive value. Its aspects are seen as phantoms and as ephemeral. Because they have no material, physical attributes, paying attention to them is an activity deemed by many to be worthless and a waste of time. But we have to remember that fantasy and imagination are the originators of everything we see that humans have created throughout time. Necessity may be called the mother of invention, but the imagination is the deity to which that mother prays in order to be given the means to invent or create. This mother of invention needs to become pregnant with the possibilities that can only come from the imagination. What this mother brings into the world owes its genesis to some creative fantasy that was allowed to gestate without interruption or limitation.

Guardian of our calling

An important function of our individual genius is its protective qualities. Many people across cultures have come to know about the concept of a guardian angel or spirit that is imbued with wisdom, foresight, and powers that are used particularly on behalf of the individual they are guarding or protecting. In contemporary times however, the healing and sustaining power of this belief is mostly dismissed by the time we reach adolescence as an empty fairy tale told to children to make them feel safe from things they don't understand.

What is little understood is that the main charge of our guardian Genius spirit is not merely to shield us from physical harm, but instead to keep our true callings safe from being lost to us through the myriad buffetings and changes we experience as we journey through our lives. The unique qualities bestowed at birth upon each individual are so precious to the creative Universal impulse that gave them to us that they are carefully guarded for us until the time that we choose to consciously turn within and make our attempt to discover and consequently express them. There is nothing more valuable in a human life than to individually express the gifts given to us at birth by the Universe, as this expression always carries the breath and fragrance of the giver itself, and is always of benefit to our fellow creatures and our collective world.

At midlife, discovering a hidden treasure that has been cared for and protected in our own consciousness throughout our life is exactly what is needed to fuel and support the rest of our earthly journey. It is at this stage in particular that many of us need to be revived by something genuine and vital in us that has been forgotten, yet carefully guarded and preserved by our Genius spirit. The knowledge that something or someone is working on our behalf in terms of helping us to deepen our sense of life purpose and meaning brings us energy, focus, and clarity.

Many Callings

One mistake we should avoid along the way to discovering our Genius qualities is to assume that we are here to express only one thing. Holding on to an idea that we are here to be solely a doctor or a musician or singularly an architect or a soldier is putting a limitation on our Genius spirit, which may have various forms of creativity to express. In my life, I have been a musician, woodworker, business owner, spiritual mentor, psychotherapist, public speaker, and writer. All of these various callings have manifested at different times in my life, and I was able to listen when they called me. The problem with clinging to the idea of a single calling is that any kind of clinging, even to one particular Genius quality, takes us out of life's flow. It is important to realize that if we feel drawn to many different things, it's okay. In following our Genius' calling, we need the freedom to change direction when necessary. What used to call to us in our early adulthood may not be the calling of the moment. Above all else, Genius always calls us in the here and now, just as we are, ready or not.

Experiment!

In order to know what our Genius qualities want to say, we will need to take chances with different ways of creative expression. We will need to experiment with whatever occurs to us in order to see what fits and what may give rise to a release of creativity. The thing about experiments is that you never know where they will lead. For this purpose, we will need to approach our Genius experiments with a gentle curiosity as well as an unbiased intention. The fact is that we should leave no stone unturned when it comes to living our true calling, because to miss out on expressing something which is innate and essential to us is to miss out on a primal sense of satisfaction and a genuine encounter with a part of our unique life purpose.

An example of responding to a call to experiment with a form of creative expression is an experience I had recently. I happened to be watching an episode of "The Voice" singing competition where Bruno Mars and his band were performing a live version of "Uptown Funk." I happen to like funk music, and actually had a funk band for a short while earlier in my life. When a certain break in the song came up, Bruno and his bandmates did a particular dance sequence that, for some reason beyond my understanding, appealed to me so much that I couldn't get it out of my head. The combination of the musical arrangement, rhythm, and dance movements fascinated something very deep in me, and I felt the need to learn the dance step. I had no practical reason for wanting this. The feeling was just there, calling to me.

The first thing to know is that I consider myself a truly terrible dancer. I have had no formal training and, dance-wise, feel terribly uncoordinated. But beyond all of that, something wanted me to learn the moves. I enlisted my wife in the experiment because she has had dance training and has a genuine aptitude for being able to see body movement and mirror it easily. Fortunately for me, she learned the moves and generously began to teach them to me. I ask you to imagine, if you care to, a 57-year-old man, untrained in dance and motivated solely by a mysterious feeling, attempting to learn the choreography to what many would call a very funky song. At first, I had to separate learning the upper body movements from learning those of the lower body, and only after much practice was I able to put the two together. I felt encouraged by the sound of the music yet, simultaneously, extremely uncoordinated. Nevertheless, the deep pull to express myself in this way was unmistakable; I had to follow it. Like the pilot, whose lack of knowing how to draw didn't matter when he was asked by the Little Prince to draw a sheep, I had to honor the mysterious request from my creative depths regardless of my lack of developed talent, what anyone thought, how it looked, or what it led to. I had a great deal of fun and was able to access and unlock some life force energy that apparently wanted to be expressed. I got to see myself from a different existential angle from engaging in this experiment. I participated in a personal mystery that rose from my unique Genius calling. Still, don't expect to see me on *Dancing with the Stars* anytime soon.

So what was this need, and why did it call me? The fact is, I simply don't need to know. In trying to know and understand an organic calling with our intellect, we take it out of the present moment where it is happening and kill part of it in the process. The things that actually make a difference in our lives are there for the sake of being there and nothing else. There can be found no justification for them, no logical reason for why or how they make a difference. They just do. Our life task is to suspend looking for the reasons why our particular Genius likes what it likes and instead draw upon our experimental natures to focus on what the Genius spirit loves to express.

In my therapy practice, clients often will reach a point of being overly informed about their personal psychology, having undergone a great deal of exploration of unconscious patterns and motivations. By wanting to know why we do what we do, we can sometimes come to an impasse that can only be traversed by simply accepting that, yes, in certain circumstances we behave in this or that habitual way. Much insight can be gained by understanding why, but time and time again, I have seen that real change comes from accepting ourselves just as we are, flaws and all, without having to know why we are the way we are. It is then that we have the freedom to move forward. Only knowing the *why* of things can keep us stuck for a long time and get in the way of what we really want to experience in our lives, which is genuine, organic change.

Needing to know the *why* can be a serious limitation to Genius' expression. Genius needs the freedom to experiment, "just because." Curiosity, impulse, need—none of these things need a reason why, and if we spend our lives waiting for that kind of answer, we run the risk of becoming professional "waiters," postponing our Genius expression until a later date when, supposedly, everything will become magically clear to us and provide us with the fortitude to step into the flow of experiential life. At midlife, we can afford to wait no longer; enough of our life has passed already, and we have no idea of how much we have left. This is reason enough to begin.

Expressing Genius

Part of successfully navigating a midlife transition is becoming open enough to allow our Genius traits to reappear in our life expression. This will take some practice, because it may have been a long time since we have spontaneously danced, sung, or written something. As with the transcendent function, as conceptualized by Jung and explained more fully in Chapter 8, when we can hold and make space for the opposing energies of "It's too late for me to learn to play the violin" and "I would really love to learn to play the violin," our consciousness presents a third thing: a solution to the dilemma that could not have been predicted or contrived. Energy is released from the unconscious as a result of acknowledging and holding the opposites, and we now have this extra energy available for consciously expressing our Genius qualities. Expressing our Genius brings us more energy and vitality instead tiring us. When we are actively engaged in our creative endeavors, we are being fed by our Genius; our alignment with it can show us that it has a limitless source of energy all of its own that we can rely on.

When approaching the topic of Genius expression, it is important to know that *how* we express our Genius is just as important as *what* we actually express. Remember that what we're going for is meaning and purpose through doing what we were meant to do. Self-satisfaction is the inner marker to be considered as opposed to an outward one such as fame or notoriety. Hence, it's not that we need to discover a new continent or develop another theory of relativity in order to follow our calling. We simply need to express whatever it is that we do in our own unique and Genius-based style.

In our earlier lives, it may have felt important to single ourselves out from the crowd by what we did. In struggling for an identity amid a sea of others who are seen as competitors, we most likely forsook our Genius connection in exchange for an ego-driven model of ourselves as separate from others and needing to reach the top of the hill before anyone else does. As we know by midlife, this approach, although sometimes successful, eventually leads to burnout, because this path involves a struggle and a fight to try stake our claim at the top of the particular hill we have chosen.

Our approach to the expression of our Genius at midlife is completely different, in that we no longer live under the illusion that we need to be the first, or the best, or the only in our expression or work. The competition element is removed, since our struggle for identity has subsided. We're basically already formed as functioning human beings by now and can get on with the task of aligning ourselves with our individual Genius, which never needed to compete because of its inbuilt sense of worthiness and integrity. We can see that there is room for everyone, since everyone's Genius is completely unique. At midlife, all of the energy spent on trying to be unique can now be used in finding what it is that we already had inside of us at birth, listening for its calling, and following it when we hear its voice.

Releasing Judgments

Judging our style of expression when we are listening to our Genius is the ultimate waste of time and energy. During this period of our lives, we are meant to express ourselves unapologetically. Without infringing on the lives of others, our task is to represent our inner uniqueness and talents outwardly, through our creative expression, not for the purpose of showing off, but for the reason of simply and finally being our genuine selves. Does a mockingbird judge herself when she sings, perched on the top of a tree? On the contrary, the song seems to come out as a necessity, which always transcends critique or judgment. We also each have our unique songs, and it is necessary for them to be sung with as much truth, conviction, and reliance on our deepest expressive inspiration as we can allow.

In order to uncover our Genius callings, you can conduct a current inventory of life expressions you are drawn to. Ask yourself the following questions, and write down the answers you receive. Don't be afraid of what comes to you, and don't judge or rule out your answers as impossible or impractical. Just give free reign to your imagination.

- What expressions am I clinging to simply because I've done them for so long?

- What, if anything do I feel is missing from my life experience?

- How will my life be different once this missing piece is found?

- What activities bring a feeling of joy when I think of them?

- What excites me at this point in my life?

- What expressions have I abandoned, thinking them impossible or impractical?

- What things don't I allow myself to express because of what others may think of me?

Take the answers that you've written down and see if any patterns emerge. You may see your Genius peeking through the spaces in your life story. It may be saying that you are on the right track, or it may indicate that you have some work to do to catch up with what it wants to express through you. You can use the information you received in this exercise as your own inner Genius guidance as to the direction to move toward. Get used to the practice of bringing your Genius out into the physical world as your creative contribution.

Gifts and Wounds

One of the salient qualities of our Genius is that of having a universal mandate to give the gifts that we have brought with us to the world. When I say "to the world," I'm indicating whatever part of the world your particular Genius is here to connect with and to touch. It may be a single child or elder. It may be a few people who are close to you — your immediate family, for instance. It may be your larger community or, in some cases, a large segment of society. How and with whom you connect depends on your Genius's particular gifts and style of giving and its unique expression.

Regardless of where we direct our gifts or how many people they eventually affect, the important thing is to situate and align ourselves internally to our Genius so that it has the opportunity to release the uniqueness it came to express. The fact is that our civilization has been created in such an interdependent way that all of us can in some way benefit from the gifts of others' Genius. Our open receiving, in turn, shines a light on our own unique Genius in order for us to find our own gifts, express them, and affect others.

Take, for example, the nonviolent protest style of Mahatma Ghandi. He cooperated with his life circumstances bringing out his Genius qualities by seeking to change 90 years of British rule in India. This expression of his Genius spirit was non-violent protest, and was met by thousands and thousands of others who, in turn, could now see a creative avenue to affect societal change that had not previously been tried. This effort to follow an aspect of a Genius path ended up by effecting a long overdue change in the lives of millions. At another end of the spectrum, I heard of an incident at a drive-through Starbucks in St. Petersburg, Florida, where one person, while paying for his own coffee at the drive up window, also paid for the person behind him in line, without the person's knowledge. When the subsequent person arrived at the window to pay, she was told that her order was already taken care

> "The world breaks everyone, and afterward, many are strong at the broken places."
> — Ernest Hemingway

of by the previous customer, and the next person in turn decided to pay for the person behind him and so on, for the next 378 customers. In contrast to Gandhi's effect on others, the Starbucks incident may seem small and insignificant. But imagine how the spark of Genius from the first person who acted from an unselfish place in concert with his Genius had, in turn, sparked a recognition in the others in line that a kind of expression other than taking care of oneself was possible. At the least, the other customers responded in kind, and I can imagine some even being inspired to do other things that occurred to them through their own Genius being activated. I, for one, was inspired by this story and tried it on my next visit to Starbucks. I have no idea if anyone else participated, but I took the opportunity to act from a place where my Genius appeared and presented itself to me by way of someone else's gift of creative imagination.

Painters, poets, writers, musicians, athletes, entrepreneurs, teachers, and doctors may have followed their Genius gifts to find their life expressions and, by doing so, opened up a channel by which those gifts are given to others. Genius gifts are greatly needed in this world. They can turn the tide of a society or the trajectory of a single life. They can have an immediate effect or take hundreds of years to take root and bear fruit in others. Whether or not this occurs doesn't matter. For some, it has become of the utmost importance to give their gifts regardless of whom they affect or when. What does matter is moving through life authentically through being who they actually are whatever the cost, as opposed to the mediocrity and inauthenticity of living through someone else's ideals or values without exploring their own innate qualities.

Using Our Genius to Heal Our Wounds

The gifts we bring to the world can be found to exist where our deepest wounding resides inside of us. We know that one of the qualities of our innate Genius is to share its gifts with the world, but what do our wounds have to do with Genius? One way to explain the connection is to look at the healing process of the human body. When we suffer a cut on our skin, several processes are triggered in our immune system in response to the wounding. Our bodies follow a series of steps to stop the bleeding, protect us from outside pathogens, and rebuild the damaged part. The wound can be seen as the activating agent that prompts the body to bring its healing gifts.

The idea with Genius is that in order to heal the wound that we have suffered, we have to give the gifts that have been unlocked in us by that wounding. In fact, a gift that is given from our own unique wounding is imbued with the energy of understanding that can penetrate another's consciousness and effect healing like nothing else. As recipients of such a gift, we know somehow that the gift is being given by someone who has been there and is either working through or has come out of the wounding as a new, more vital person. We feel that we can trust this person because, somehow, he or she can see our wounds and authentically address them.

The Wounded Healer

A Greek myth portrays a centaur named Chiron who had experienced deep physical and psychological wounding at an early age. He was rejected by his own mother, the goddess Philyra, and he grew up under the care of his adopted father Apollo. Apollo, the god of music, prophecy, poetry, and healing, taught everything he knew to Chiron, who become a healer of men. Due to his need to heal himself, he was imbued with a wealth of the empathy and compassion needed to effect change or healing in others.

Regarding healing through our wounding, in his book, *The Wounded Healer*, Henri Nouwen says,

> A wounded healer is someone who can listen to a person in pain without having to speak about his or her own wounds. When we have lived through a painful depression, we can listen with great attentiveness and love to a depressed friend without mentioning our experience. Mostly it is better not to direct a suffering person's attention to ourselves. We have to trust that our own bandaged wounds will allow us to listen to others with our whole beings. That is healing.

Everyone on earth, especially by midlife has had the experience of a deep wounding of some sort or another. Whether caused by an emotional or physical blow, these wounds have become internalized and largely repressed in our unconscious, yet subsequently affect our actions on a daily basis. Psychologically, we either respond to the wounds that we see others carrying that remind us of our own wounds, or we react in the opposite way and try to avoid seeing those wounds in others because we're still afraid to see them in ourselves. The difference between a response and a reaction is that the qualities of a response come from being sensitive to our own Genius being touched by something, whereas a reaction is about not being ready to heal our own wound and, by ignoring the messages of our Genius, not yet allowing it to have its creative say,.

My own example of responding to others wounds as a psychotherapist comes from a period of deep depression in my life that I never imagined I would experience. It was the most confusing and disorienting experience I had ever had, and it shook my basic idea of myself down to the ground. The time I spent in the anxiety and panic of losing an identity attached to a working self or life schema at midlife manifested PTSD symptoms that took a great deal of effort by many compassionate others on my behalf to bring me through. Although I had counseled others for most of my adult life, helping them through their various life challenges, I now felt an intense need to return to graduate school at age 50 to obtain a masters degree in counseling psychology. Now when I see someone in my office who is experiencing a depression or symptoms of a trauma, I recognize my own wounds and am able to use my Genius traits to help guide someone else's healing and recovery.

Genius plays a major role in any healing situation regarding life purpose, meaning, and individual expression. In her forward to Gabrielle Roth's book *Maps to Ecstasy*, cultural anthropologist Angeles Arrien writes about the beginning of the healing process in Shamanic societies. If an individual goes to see a Shaman for help with depression, for instance, some of the things the Shaman will ask are *"When did you stop singing? When did you stop dancing? When did you stop being enchanted by stories? When did you stop finding comfort in the sweet territory of silence?"*

The answers to these questions may indicate an area of an individual's life where he or she has "lost soul," or a connection to an essential part of their basic identity. When we discover that we have curtailed the natural expressions of soul, Genius gives us clues as to where we can pick them up again and allow them in our lives. We can take the terms *singing, dancing, enchanted by stories,* and *comfort in silence* to have both literal and metaphoric meanings. All of these represent qualities that transcend society and culture and point to the inbuilt necessity to engage in creative expression of some kind. This creative expression comes forth in response to a deeper impetus, the voice of our personal Genius, which, when acknowledged and honored in our lives, has the power to heal us of our deep sense of loss and grieving. The guiding spirit of Genius can return an element that is essential to our experience of ourselves: the sacred nature of our individual life expression. When we truly see our lives as sacred, as gifts that have been given to us by the universe, our healing has begun and will bring inner depth and rewards that nothing else can bring.

The scars we carry on our skin are the strongest patches of flesh on our bodies. Likewise, the psychic and emotional scarring of our personal wounds are sources of an inner strength. Giving this strength to others in whatever form that flows naturally from our Genius invites further healing of our own wounds. The dance of Genius is thus a healing dance for all involved. Whether one person is affected or millions, the important thing is to engage in this dance in order to be in step with our Genius gifts.

4

Midlife and Liminal Space

One of the hallmarks of finding ourselves in a midlife transition is the sense of living in-between worlds. We have operated under what can be called our young world view up until now, and we're finding that our ideas and conclusions about life and what is important to us are no longer applicable to the challenges and situations we currently experience. This period of living in the special space between one life paradigm and another, one life vision and another, is an important stage in our life development. We are living in *liminal space*, that is, living in a space between two worlds—no longer in the old one, but not yet in the new one. This space of not knowing who we are or who we're becoming is actually an auspicious time to encounter and engage with our Genius spirit.

During this time of living in between, we are seeing things not in the daylight of the fully risen sun but by a different kind of light, a lunar light, whereby everything takes on a dreamlike quality. For a long time, the sun cast long shadows in our younger life, when we lived outwardly. Now is the time to explore those shadows of ourselves, the choices we made, and the actions we took. Moonlight is a softer light where the imagination is freed to wander through the landscape of metaphor, where there is more room for ambiguity and nuance in a poetic reenvisioning of ourselves, of where we've been, and of where we are going. Liminal space is a world where a second gestation occurs and where we are preparing for a type of second birth, into our new life.

Once we have found ourselves in this place between worlds, we can either fight with it and insist that we move directly into our new lives in the clear sunlight, or we can use this time for what it is intended: a time for rest and reflection, for revisiting long abandoned dreams and passions, and for embracing the parts of ourselves that were forced into the shadow of our consciousness while we became practical people who needed to provide, perform, and achieve. This liminal place is a refuge from those concretized things. Its purpose is to allow us to reencounter our unformed selves without any justification for why we're doing so. Here we can be free to be impractical for the sake of creativity. We can indulge an unexplainable emotion. We can draw sustenance from the deep unconscious well of existence where possibility dwells.

Due to our societal and cultural habit of engaging in black-and-white thinking, we desperately need this time and place to be shaken loose from concrete ideas of ourselves. Here, things are more fluid and mysterious. The outlines of things are blurred and permeable. Reaching for certainty in the liminal world is like trying to grasp a fistful of water. Our only responsibility when we find ourselves living here is to allow ourselves this time simply to not know what is happening. Trying to make logical sense of this time can be maddening. Instead, this period can be experienced as a soul vacation or mental sabbatical from a life that has gone as far as it can go in one direction.

In liminal space, we can receive a different type of nourishment that will prepare us for our new life. Like our time spent in our mother's womb, where we were fed with nutrients that strengthened and prepared our physical bodies and all of their systems for the challenges that life would certainly bring, our time in the liminal womb is preparing us with what we will need to thrive in our new environment. This process can't be rushed, but the quickest way to be born into our new world is to let go into what is happening to and for us now, and let it do its work.

Encountering Genius in Liminal Space

For the most part, the Genius spirit inside of us has been relegated to and occasionally encountered in our unconscious world: the world of dreams, memories, and fantasies. Whenever a part of us is blocked from expressing itself in our conscious life, it will express itself nonetheless somewhere else, namely in our unconscious world that speaks to us through metaphor and symbol. Remember that our Genius spirit is a part of us, no less than our hands and feet, or our blood and our hearts. We cannot separate ourselves from the talents and qualities that our Genius carries with it any more than we can separate the marrow from our bones and still be a living human being. Naturally, these qualities and attributes that are inseparable from our Genius are also inseparable from our consciousness.

As I said before, the time we spend in the liminal space between two worlds is an excellent time to encounter and engage with our Genus spirit. Through conscious attunement to its metaphoric messages we can allow a space for the gifts it wants to manifest to bubble up into our consciousness and be integrated into our daily lives. In this way, we are actively participating in the process of our Genius spirit's qualities and the energy they contribute to our outward expression in the physical world.

One way of beginning the process of engaging with our Genius that many explorers of consciousness have used is to create, in a physical form such as a drawing, painting, sculpture, dance or movement, song or poem, or other artistic medium, an image of one of the Genius qualities we discover in our inner explorations. Bringing what was once hidden and nebulous into physical reality can help to integrate our unconscious and conscious worlds. This integration brings a boost of psychic energy through expressing a suppressed creative impulse. This psychic energy is then consciously available to us. We can now use the energy it was taking to keep our Genius talents in the unconscious to create unique and unexpected forms of expression that are more in harmony with our sense of individual life purpose and meaning. These expressions that we manifest in our physical world carry with them the potency of the world of image and symbol and maintain a mysterious and unexplainable living presence of that world long after they have been created.

I once had a dream in which I found myself arriving late for a meeting where matters of the soul were being discussed. I had brought with me a small, round, silver medallion with markings around the outer edge. I explained that the reason I was late was because I had been creating this medallion for the past 3 days, and that it was the symbol of the last 30 years of my life.

I awoke from this dream with the image of the medallion, and it remained with me for many months. The image felt so important that I decided to create a model of it and have it cast in silver in order to manifest this dream image into physical reality. Before I had begun to create my model, I had a mysterious and synchronistic experience while attending a weekend of classes at my graduate school. I arrived back at my room after a morning class to discover an assortment of seashells that a fellow student had found that morning on the beach and had arranged on a shelf in my room as a surprise. In the center of the arrangement sat a sea-washed clay poker chip, which she had also found washed up on the beach. It was the exact image of the medallion in my dream! I was filled with a sense of awe and wonder at how this could possibly happen—how something from my dream world had connected and expressed itself in my physical life.

As an active, conscious act of participation in this phenomenon, I had the poker chip/medallion cast in silver and carried it in my pocket as a talisman that represented a condensation of the last 30 years of my life. At the time, it was important to remember those years as something valuable and worthwhile, and the medallion helped to remind me in times of self-doubt and confusion regarding that period of my life. Additionally, and to further this expression, after I had honored my past by carrying this silver symbol for a few years, I felt the need to express my future and the potential that it held. I envisioned it as somehow golden, and gathered some pieces of gold jewelry that had had deep symbolic meanings to me—my deceased parents' wedding rings, a gold coin from my wife, a gold cross that I used to wear—and had them melted down to create a gold version of the medallion, which I carry to this day. It reminds me of the immense possibility that exists by bringing out the unique qualities of my inborn Genius.

Chronos and Kairos

At midlife, we become (sometimes painfully) aware of how much time has passed in our lives as well as realizing that the unknown but finite quantity of time left to live into the future is really not under our control. The concept and realities of time can therefore take on an important role in our midlife identities. It follows, then, that many of us have the deep realization that the quality of our time left is more important than the quantity, since there seems to be something we can actually do to affect it.

The ancient Greeks had two different words for time: *chronos* and *kairos*. Chronos is chronological time. This kind of time passes from one day to another, one experience to another, and its minutes and days can be measured and counted. Chronos is quantitative, steady, and predictable time. It keeps everything in order and in its proper place. The other word for time, kairos, is more of a timeless time or rather a point or experience when time seems to stand still. Its essence is qualitative, and so the emphasis is on *what* takes place there rather than *how long* it took to happen. Kairos is the moment of opportunity or perfect timing of something happening, which a person can either be present to and benefit from or miss and experience a sense of regret. Being consciously awake and available during a kairos moment is what ultimately effects lasting change in us and is an excellent opportunity to encounter Genius. Our Genius speaks in a timeless, poetic language that can only be understood and integrated in kairos time. Because our Genius qualities are perennial and don't age with our bodies, they are an eternal component of our inner makeup that often are revealed when we forget about the counting of the days and the sleepy routines that fill those days.

Understanding kairos is especially valuable in midlife, when we both remember and are on the lookout for experiences that take us out of a linear, chronos time and instead suspend us in the present moment, a timeless moment where an opportunity for tremendous growth in consciousness can occur. At midlife, having had the experience of being fully present to some, but not all of our kairos moments, we can become keenly aware, sensitive, and ready for this type of time to appear along with the transformational qualities and potential it can birth. When we reflect back on our life experience, we can realize that these very moments of timelessness are what have changed us the most throughout our lives and that their reverberations often last until we take our last breath, and possibly beyond that.

An experience of kairos I remember occurred one day during a check-in in one of my classes in graduate school. My turn came to share about what was going on for me at that point in my life, and I explained that my company had just made a large sale from which I was going to benefit financially. I mentioned that it was difficult for me to acknowledge any accomplishments I might make, due to the religious indoctrination I had received early on in my life about the need to be humble and not claim achievements as my own. I had accepted the dogma that everything "is done by God" and that it was hubris for the selfish ego to take any credit for something that might result from an individual effort. At that point in my check-in, the professor stopped the class and had everyone in my cohort stand up and applaud, acknowledging my accomplishment. I entered kairos. Chronological time had stopped, and I was suspended in a timeless place where I had to acknowledge inwardly that a large group of people were singularly expressing their congratulations specifically to me. I felt my resistance to accepting compliments and the accompanying embarrassment fading away, and I wanted to weep at the great empathy and compassion shown by my professor, who recognized that a moment had presented itself as an opportunity to heal something in a person standing in front of him. To this day, I can still feel an incredible sense of gratitude for that experience. In the state of kairos, I had plenty of timeless space to experience it fully, giving my entire attention to it so as to be transformed in some way.

How do we make ourselves available to this timeless, auspicious moment when all things come together? I truly believe that kairos is actually available at any time we allow ourselves to be moved by something. We just need to increase our capacity to perceive it. If we are truly present to a sunset, a falling leaf, or a kind look from another person, we can be changed. Being inwardly available to be changed into a more authentic version of ourselves sets the stage for kairos to penetrate our chronological lives and meet us at any point along the way.

Genius is always concerned with quality over quantity. In fact, the quality of our unique Genius traits is what makes them singularly unique. There will only ever be one of each of us, and the chronological time we spend making the effort to allow for kairos time to appear is the path of this uniqueness. Our Genius can appear in kairos time and make its desires for our fulfillment known to us. It is our job to recognize and remember how it feels in those sparkling moments where everything comes together under the protection of our Genius, and new possibilities are seen as being very close at hand.

Religiousness

"Among all my patients in the second half of life —
that is to say, over thirty-five — there has not been
one whose problem in the last resort was not that
of finding a religious outlook on life. It is safe to
say that every one of them fell ill because he had
lost what the living religions of every age have
given their followers, and none of them has been
really healed who did not regain his
religious outlook."
— *Carl Jung*

Religion can be a touchy subject for many people, but tracing the word *religion* back to its source, we find that one interpretation comes from the Latin word *religare* which means "to fasten or bind fast," particularly in relation to the bond between humans and gods. The religious outlook that Jung refers to is thus a reconnection of humans with the numinous or sacred aspect of themselves from which they have somehow become disconnected. In terms of the Genius spirit, this means that there are as many forms of religion or "fastening back to the sacred" as there are individuals. In other words, each of us must find our own religiousness for ourselves, whether it lies within the framework of one of the major religious traditions or is something uniquely our own. It could also be comprised of a combination of the two. The important thing here is for us to have a connection with something naturally occurring in us that supersedes our patterns of thought and can help lift us to a level of awareness above the ingrained and outdated beliefs about ourselves that we have developed by midlife. These outdated beliefs can feel like a stone that we carry around our necks, rendering us unable to respond to our daily challenges in a consciously active way. Our old beliefs of ourselves have worn out, and are no longer serving us as they used to. It is time for us to clean house.

My effort to engage in my own religiousness from the ages of 20 to 50 was in the form of an Eastern-based model of transcendental meditation practice. Although this practice was intensely rewarding for a time, after around 20 years, my practice had become largely a dry exercise that I tried to muscle my way through with pure discipline for the next 10 years. I had become stuck in an idea of enlightenment that was no longer serving me. However, because I was a mentor and teacher in a spiritual community, it was extremely difficult to change. The practice that was supposed to be freeing me had become a seemingly beautiful trap in which I lived. For the benefit of others in my community, my life was set up to be a model and example of how to be a devoted practitioner of meditation. After spending so much time publicly speaking about enlightenment and awakening, how was I supposed to reconcile the fact that I was experiencing a stagnation of consciousness? I was no longer enjoying the benefits of growth that I had previously experienced, and I was desperately trying to "manage" this existential crisis by more meditation and devotional practices.

Luckily, the group finally broke apart amid revelations of the main teacher's corruption, manipulation, and deceptions, and life unceremoniously spit me out into the world, unencumbered by my role as a teacher. However, with this "generosity" coming to me at midlife, I experienced the simultaneous losses of faith, vocation, community, life purpose, and meaning. For quite a while, I was adrift in a state of confusion and depression from which I had no energy to free myself. The old methods weren't working, and nothing was presented to me that could take their place. It was time for my "dark night of the soul," and I have to say that it got really, really dark.

After the darkness had served its purpose of cleansing me of what was old, worn out, and limiting, I began again to find a sense of religiousness that actually fit with my current state of consciousness and identity. It became an engaging and rewarding process of continued growth and development for me, and finding aspects of my Genius along the way both encourages and inspires me to keep going.

Following our Genius instincts and traits requires a willingness to move into the flow of the present and eternal dance of life. Because we are living beings, and the experience of life's vitality depends on movement and flow, it is necessary for us to reconnect to a state of consciousness that has this freedom of movement—one that is agile and responsive, residing in this present moment just as it is. Luckily, this state is available to all of us individually at any time. Its qualities appear when we are willing to suspend our old way of being just long enough for something fresh and unique to penetrate our consciousness.

Remember that, in terms of our unique Genius being underutilized for this purpose, we have a very large and integral part of ourselves—*our genuine callings*—that has been sending us messages in the form of the symptoms of dissatisfaction, vague yearnings, and restlessness. If we can listen to and heed the importance of these messages by actually doing something to address them, our intrinsic Genius qualities of curiosity, exploration, and enthusiasm can enter into the whole of our life experience and change our trajectory. The changes that spring from Genius, however disturbing, somehow turn out to be necessary and good.

Finding our own sense of religiousness and tending to it regularly brings an added dimension to our lives that nothing else can provide. From this state, we are free to wonder, imagine, dream, and create a fuller and more holistic life. Taking this opportunity creates a space for our Genius to emerge and express the qualities of ourselves that are meant to bring immense satisfaction to our life experience. We become deeper and richer individuals by giving credence to what is invisible to the outward eyes of others but increasingly tangible and genuinely real to our individual interiority.

Finding a Sense of Religiousness

In order to "fasten" ourselves to what is sacred to us, we will need to locate and identify the things that have happened in our lives that have inspired and transported us, however briefly, into kairos or timeless time. These experiences provide the clues that will help us locate our personal religiousness that exists in that timeless, sacred place.

To help to identify and remember these experiences, we can ask ourselves these questions and take note of the answers we receive:

- When did you experience your first moment that seemed to transport you into a timeless place? This would be your first "aha" moment or "mini enlightenment" about something.

- Where were you at the time, both physically and mentally?

- What messages were imparted to you, and what did you realize about yourself or about your life that sticks with you to this day?

- Did you put these realizations into action in your daily life?

- If you have taken action, has this changed your daily life experience?

- If you haven't, what else is needed to motivate you to act?

The extent to which we listen to and incorporate the gifts that appear as revelations to us, however small they may seem at the time, is the level of importance we place on our religiousness or sense of the sacred. As we become quieter and more sensitive to our inner workings, we experience more of these naturally occurring timeless moments, and we come to see that soul and Genius are always speaking and expressing in their own voices. We begin to recognize these voices not as anonymous messages from a mysterious "somewhere else" but as actual parts of ourselves that have always been there — sacred, precious, and unique.

Sacred Practice

In order to benefit from our own sense of the sacred, and if we want to include honoring our Genius spirit, we need to make a time each day to engage in a conscious acknowledgement of it. An aspect of the meaning of the word *sacred* is to "set apart" something for a higher purpose. The time we set apart serves as our "practice" and can take such forms as prayer, meditation, affirmations, or active imagination. Some of us find a quiet morning or evening walk to be the best medium for acknowledging the sacred, while others may drink tea in silence as a technique. Whatever method we find that personally serves to help us remember and focus our attention on our sense of the sacred every day will benefit us in the long run.

Acknowledging the sacred is the act of expanding the awareness of ourselves and of what comprises us as individuals. It is extremely encouraging to encounter parts of ourselves that are mysterious, surprising, expansive, and illuminating. When we devote a regular time to acknowledging the sacred aspects of ourselves, we are opening up a reservoir of energy that can carry us through even the most difficult times we may come to experience.

For 30 plus years, I used a form of silent transcendental meditation as my regular practice of acknowledging the sacred. However, after experiencing my dark night of the soul, this type of meditation was just not working to inspire me anymore. I had to find a different way of acknowledging what was sacred in me *now*. We may find that as we grow and change, different ways of practicing sacredness will need to be found. This is completely natural, given that as we continue to grow consciously, different ways to acknowledge our deeper selves will make more sense to us. Remember that whatever brings us into the present moment and gives us a sense of peace and stillness can be our practice. Currently, my practice is to get up early, around two hours before sunrise, make some tea, and sit quietly for a few minutes. Since I am in the flow of writing this book on Genius, I invite my Genius spirit to give me an image that is the seed of what I will write about that morning. I deliberately "get out of the way" and allow this image to appear in my consciousness. When the image appears, I hold it in my awareness and allow it to unfold into words, and then I write them down. I'm not doing automatic writing or acting as a medium. On the contrary, I become an active participant, using my writing skills in conjunction with the inspiration I receive from the depths of my consciousness. I become engaged in my own process of the sacred.

Making time and space to be grateful

Many of us have the tendency to live for an ideal. In whatever context we choose, whether we choose the ideal of monetary success, fame and recognition, sharing a loving relationship, or maintaining optimum physical health, we use it as a goal or marker set somewhere in the future to measure ourselves against. The idea is that when we reach that ultimate goal, only then will we be experiencing what we should be experiencing, and our lives will fall into balance as a result. Living for an ideal has two main drawbacks:

1. It allows us to postpone feeling whole and complete until sometime in the future.

2. It keeps us in the endless exercise of comparing ourselves to others for our sense of worth.

Both of these aspects serve to keep us waiting for something else to happen in order to feel satisfied, fulfilled, or hopeful about ourselves. Whatever or wherever we find ourselves right now never quite mirrors the ideal and can consequently be a source of shame and frustration for us. Our creative energies are all but used up in the spiral of everything that comes from never quite making the mark.

The problem with this approach to our lives is in the postponement of enjoying what is happening right now in deference to the idea of how great it will be in the future when we reach our ideal. Remember that feeling frustrated and shameful in not being where we think we should be in life diverts a great deal of our precious life energy that we desperately need in order to fuel our creative path forward. The one thing, above all, that we can't afford at midlife is wasting more time not living our purposeful and meaningful lives.

In order to see our lives objectively as having value in the here and now, we may need to use our Genius' creativity to exercise a daily practice of noticing things that actually work out — our daily victories, successes, and good fortune — even in the presence of not having reached our ultimate goal or ideal. The fallacy inherent in the concept of reaching an ideal is that we will finally be able to rest from our consistent efforts when we finally get there. We don't allow ourselves to lift our noses up from the daily grindstone we're turning in order to see that many things do work out and that we are given small or large victories and successes every day. If we are to create a deeply rewarding and balanced life of meaning and purpose, we will have to develop the knack of taking regular intervals of rest from our work in order to acknowledge deeply the things that are working out for us.

Engaging in this practice can put our lives in balance as far as seeing more realistically that our lives are made up of both failures and successes, each taking their turn on the stage of our experience but never as solo performers. Our failures and successes encounter and interact with one another. When we let go of the ideal as our life-marker, we can begin to acknowledge both players and give them their turns in the spotlight. Since most of us have no problem acknowledging the performances of our failures and shortcomings, our efforts would be well spent on addressing our daily victories and successes, large and small, in an effort to see our lives more realistically and less ideally.

Awareness of Success Exercise

One of the first things that we can notice every day is the state of our health. When we wake up in the morning, we can acknowledge some basic things and be appreciative of them. Remember that this is not simply an exercise of positivity but instead of seeing what actually takes place daily from which you can draw a sense of strength, stamina, and gratitude.

- Take a second to focus on a part of your body that actually feels good. Chances are you will find quite a few places, but because health never calls attention to itself like disease does, you may have to look closely. See that part as functioning perfectly and serving you and your quest for purpose.

- As you have your morning meal, notice that right now, you are taken care of and that you've been given a way to sustain and fuel your body for another day.

- Notice to what extent you can move. Not taking movement for granted is extremely important because it allows you to exercise your individualism and autonomy.

Throughout your day, in whatever kind of work you do, you can again use your awareness to witness the things that don't specifically call out to you, because they simply work out naturally.

- If you travel to work, did you arrive in one piece?

- Be aware of how the day brings its own challenges and tasks that you meet and accomplish, however small they may seem. Remember that all of these small accomplishments add up.

- Completing work for the day, allow it to be enough for now. Come back to your nonworking self and notice the shift in mental focus. Take an inventory of how many large and small things worked out today.

Coming home from work, you may feel tired or fatigued from the day's efforts. This is actually a good thing, as it signals that you are ready to move into a different space of being where physical or mental effort and problem solving is no longer the focus.

- Allow yourself to shift gears into nonworking mode. See if you are able to do so, and notice what happens in your consciousness. Acknowledge that the world is taking care of itself right now.

- Take some time to enjoy actively something that you like to do. Notice that you are able to engage with that thing in the present moment, and realize that you are not shirking your responsibilities to your job, family, or community by enjoying something for yourself.

When it is time for bed, you may already be thinking about tomorrow's challenges. Besides resting your body for the night, you can let your mental and emotional concerns rest by focusing on the natural transition of the earth and the quiet of the night that have been gifted to you.

- Close your eyes and take stock of the happenings of your day. Acknowledge the fact that you are still here and that your daily work has been done, to whatever extent.

- As your body lies down to rest, notice that your body systems are functioning and that you have a place to relax and recharge throughout the night.

- See how you have successfully navigated through another day and that by acknowledging this success, you are bringing your active awareness to the reality of what happens daily and allowing space for more victories to take place.

Remember that bringing awareness to something that you have previously ignored can release energy that has been stuck around that thing and that you will be able to use that released energy in new ways. By acknowledging the small things that actually work on a daily basis, you can free yourself from the falsehood that you are not successful as a person. In fact, no "large" successes would be possible were it not for the basic successes of your life that so consistently happen that you hardly notice them.

Being successful is ultimately about inner integrity and character. Worldly accomplishments may occur, and fame, recognition, and monetary success may result, but the sense of purpose that you seek at midlife will come from living as an individual (one who is no longer divided within oneself), with the strength of character that can endure its failures and acknowledge its successes equally.

Individuation

The idea that we are genuinely unique individuals at our core is a great and useful one. But if we follow along with this idea in terms of self-actualizing our uniqueness, by midlife we can see that it doesn't happen by accident; it involves a process that requires our conscious participation.

The word *individual* comes from the Latin word *individuus*, meaning "undivided, unfragmented, or whole." Jung's concept of individuation can be described as the lifelong process of becoming who we were meant to be as individuals. Through our life experiences and our conscious awareness of the impact of those experiences on our psyche, we are on a constant journey to wholeness. Jung saw individuation as a natural, universal process, taking place to whatever degree in everyone and everything. When we were born, we were our unique selves in seed form, and everything that happens to us is in some way meant to help the seed grow into its fullest potential.

Individuation at Midlife

By the time midlife arrives, we have had innumerable life experiences that have affected us on countless levels of our existence, and the ways in which we have reacted and responded to those experiences can be said to have shaped our identities up until this point. So far, so good, so to speak. However, another dimension to our experience is required at midlife to continue the individuation process, because it is no longer simply about outer experiences shaping our personalities. As we reach the second half of life, we must inwardly engage the individuation process as active participants, bringing our awareness and attention to the endeavor; we become co-creators of our path to wholeness. Willingly applying our conscious effort to seeing both the light and dark aspects of who we have become up until now, we will need to develop the capacity to embrace and integrate them into our identity. The first half of life is about embracing an ideal of who we are and where we are going. This is to embrace the singular. In the second half of life, individuation requires that we embrace the duality: both the light and dark realities of who we are now. This task is more complex than the first because we are required to abandon the sense of safety that clinging to an ideal can bring. For the sake of uncovering ourselves as genuine human beings, complete with flaws, shortcomings, and persistent habits, we will need to admit that we have fallen short of our youthful ideals somewhere along the way. What at first glance may appear as a failure of achievement turns out to be the perfect situation for us to deepen and ripen as individuals, which is the hallmark task during the second half of life. We have not failed; we have learned the true nature of an ideal, that in following its light, it creates a shadow in us that we now will have to integrate into our self identity if we are to continue to grow and truly individuate.

I remember having lunch with the director of a halfway house for emotionally disturbed children where I was working in my early 20s. She was showing me a pair of expensive sunglasses she had bought in Europe on a recent ski trip. The lenses were noticeably scratched and scraped. Her daughter, sitting next to her, had a pair of the same sunglasses and pointed out to us that her lenses were still in pristine shape. I remember thinking how unfortunate it was that my boss's sunglasses were damaged. The director, seeing my look of disappointment, simply said: "Ah, yes. I've had to learn to live with myself!" This small remark and the way it was said left an indelible mark on my psyche that I was only able to comprehend when I reached midlife. It now means to me that life is not a perfect situation to be reached someday by keeping a shiny ideal consistently intact but instead a journey made more interesting by including our flaws, shortcomings, and failures as parts of ourselves that carry their own intrinsic importance.

The focus of our younger lives is to live the *ideal* of self, work, family, and accomplishments; in other words, living for the goal at the end of the path or journey. The orientation of the second half of our lives is to the journey itself. By now, most of us have learned that the journey is where all of the interesting stuff happens. We are living and breathing for the moment-to-moment experiences along the way, having realized that the ideal that was necessary before is to us, at midlife, a phantom and an illusion that never delivers the goods. It is simply not acceptable any more to postpone our lives because we haven't attained an imagined magical situation. We're only right here, now, roots in the earth, branches in the sky. And it's good.

Taking out the trash

"There is an answer in a question
And there is hope within despair
And there is beauty in a failure
And there are depths beyond compare
There is a role of a lifetime
And there's a song yet to be sung
And there's a dumpster in the driveway
Of all the plans that came undone"
Death Cab for Cutie
"Black Sun" lyrics

One of the knacks that it is important to continue to develop every day is to engage in the ritual disposal of the psychological and emotional material that is no longer of use to us. A daily practice of unburdening ourselves of all sorts of things that don't serve our purpose of self-discovery or moving forward with our life journey is an essential ingredient to uncovering our Genius.

This practice can be seen as a continuous clearing of our waking consciousness in order for us to approach our moment-to-moment experiences with a fresh perspective. Countless experiences have and will continue to take place throughout our lifetimes; a spectrum of inner impressions and our myriad reactions to all of them. Our reactions and responses to these experiences however leave a psychological residue in our consciousness that often requires an effort on our parts to clear out. This residue can be seen as the "wrapping paper" that our experiences came in. Over time, as our reactions to the outward appearance of a particular experience subside, we are able to focus on what was inside the wrapping. As responsible and sincere people, we always want to get the import of the gifts we've been given by life, since this acceptance and integration is what changes and deepens us as individuals. However, by midlife most of us have mistakenly saved all of the wrapping paper our gifts came in as well. When life sends us a lesson or experience, we initially react to the wrapping, which we may entitle "tragedy", or "trauma", "luck" or "reward". The midlife expertise we will need to exercise is to divest ourselves of this wrapping or psychic residue that encircled the gifts of experience that have come to us and simply keep the essence contained inside. This essence is devoid of judgments, conclusions, or comparisons to others' gifts. Above all, the essence of our gifts always points somewhere. They indicate further movement on our part. They are a beckoning and an invitation to go forward. Our job then, is to separate the packaging from the product and deposit the trash at the curb every day. In this way we end up with the pure messages we were intended to receive from life and the universe without having to wade through a gigantic heap of "shoulds", "could haves", "this must means", and "I cant's.

The trash that can be discarded can include such daily occurrences as succumbing to an old habit, arguing with a friend or lover, making a regrettable mistake, or the residual feelings left over from simply having a "bad day". The idea behind this "tending to" our trash is to ritualize our daily purging of failures, shortcomings and "bad fortune" in order to make space in our inner worlds for new and potentially rewarding and invigorating experiences to take place. When our inner palette is stained with the colors of the past, and with impressions of all of the expressions and experiences that didn't quite work out the way we wished they would, we need a daily cleansing of our waking consciousness so that the fresh and new creative impulses we receive from our Genius aren't seen through a dirty existential lens. It is our job as creative participants in our lives to give ourselves the cleanest houses we can by taking the trash from our near and distant past to the curb. When we throw out our trash in this conscious and deliberate way, we are creating space for new life-giving experiences. For instance, throwing the lingering shame of a former addiction to alcohol on the trash heap makes more room for creative expression around that issue. This experience of addiction now having been lived through, and its accompanying psychological residue discarded consciously can allow valuable character-filled information to emerge that can affect the lives of others whom we encounter in a profound and genuine way.

More Than Happiness

From the standpoint of Genius, happiness is not singularly the ultimate goal of life. Happiness is simply a byproduct of living a life of meaning and purpose. It is the fruit of the tree of fulfillment. It is a naturally occurring phenomenon that is a result of living an authentic life.

Most of us have used the technique of trying to create the proper circumstances that will make happiness appear, such as attempting to acquire money, job security, and lasting relationships or by buying houses and building businesses. We have chased the things that promise happiness when we finally have them. In the meantime, as we wait for happiness to appear, we get glimpses and fleeting moments of it, and eventually return to our waiting process. The promise of happiness as our ultimate goal creates a willingness in us to endure years and years of unhappiness and struggle for its sake. In Genius terms, this methodology is backward-facing. By embracing our Genius spirit, the idea is that when our lives are full of meaning and creative purpose from listening to our inbuilt tendencies and callings, happiness is experienced naturally and *precedes* our circumstances. We can't always be the winner, we can't always succeed at everything we try. But we are happy when our Genius is being lived, because we are fully engaged in the life we came here to express.

Seeking happiness alone is like us living as ugly ducklings, so out of place and confused, only to find that happiness comes as a result of realizing our true nature as swans. Everything becomes clear to us when we honor what we already are. We need not create circumstances to attract happiness. We only need to allow the seed of our Genius to grow into what it was meant to be in the first place. Seeing our life's journey in this way, an authentic life full of purpose and meaning is the goal, while happiness comes along for the ride.

As you can see, this approach may involve a radical shift of focus for many of us. After all, the phrase *pursuit of happiness* is even written in the United States Declaration of Independence as an unalienable right. However, the word *pursuit* suggests that happiness may be an elusive creature; we may chase it without ever capturing it. We may never ultimately arrive at its door. When we shift our focus to finding our individual life's unique meaning and purpose through responding to our true callings provided by our Genius qualities, we are no longer pursuing happiness for its sake alone; we find it when we don't chase after it, because it no longer eludes us. It is given to us as a gift of existence, not as a reward for hard work, but as a homecoming gift when we dwell with our Genius and are responding to its clear and persistent calling to us.

Whatever it takes for us to make the shift from only pursuing happiness to listening to our Genius callings is what our focus should be. Take this happiness inventory to see in which ways you try and find happiness and the circumstances you're trying manifest to bring that happiness about.

Pursuit of Happiness Inventory

- List several things that you currently think will make you ultimately happy.

- What circumstances will need to be present to produce this happiness?

- How long have you been trying to create these circumstances?

- Have you succeeded in creating any of these circumstances?

- Have you become consistently happy because of their existence?

- If so, see if some of the circumstances are tied to a sense of meaning and purpose.

- If not, take note of your ideas about the next round of circumstances that will really bring happiness this time.

- See if you gain any insights from observing how this process is working in your life.

When you finally realize that you have only been chasing the *idea* of happiness, you see the need to stop living *once-removed* from a dynamic experience of your life and, instead, engage in what is calling to you from your Genius spirit to express. There is a state of fulfillment that comes from listening and responding to your inner Genius guide. Happiness will be there as well, curious and excited as to what may happen next.

Eudaimonia

Another word for the Genius spirit comes from the Latin word *daemon*, literally meaning "spirit." To further this translation and meaning, the Greek form of the word is *daimon*, which translates as a "guiding spirit," "genius," or "giver of fortune." It was only later, with subsequent religious writings, that this spelling was changed to *demon*, redefining the word, for one political reason or another, as a "fiend" or "devil." Given the earlier versions of the concept of Genius, for the purpose of uncovering our Genius, we will need to expand our understanding of this guardian/gift giving indwelling spirit not as some foreign entity inhabiting our bodies against our will but as a naturally occurring feature in each and every human being.

The Greeks used another word: *eudaimonia*. In contemporary definitions, *eudaimonia* simply can be explained as happiness. However, *eudaimonia*, as defined in the *Encyclopedia Britannica*, means being in "the state of having a good indwelling spirit, a good genius." Tracing this idea farther back in history, Aristotle, while writing his *Nicomachean Ethics*, originally coined the term *eudaimonia* as representing the highest good in man. The highest good, according to Aristotle wasn't, in fact, simply happiness, feeling great, or satisfying our appetites, which are circumstantial states that can come and go, but instead, the virtuous striving to achieve what is the best in us. Carol Ryff, in her research on psychological wellbeing and aging, explains Aristotle's *eudaimonia* in this way:

> Eudaimonia thus captured the essence of the two great Greek imperatives: first, to know yourself, and second, to become what you are. The latter requires discerning one's unique talents (the daimon that resides in us all), and then working to bring them to reality.

Another way of looking at the idea is mythologist Michael Meade's description of eudaimonia as doing and being what makes our Genius happy. The concept is that when we are expressing our Genius talents and qualities in the world, we are fulfilling, in the deepest sense of the word, our *calling* or inbuilt *vocation*. This feeling of fulfillment, purpose, and life meaning comes from allowing our Genius' gifts to be given, as an unburdening of our inborn talents that are meant to be given away. At midlife, if we haven't yet moved into the state of bringing our inbuilt Genius talents to a full expression, we feel the uncomfortable yearnings of a life not fully lived.

Remember that our Genius qualities were born with us. As much as it seems that we have to strive to bring them out, their natural tendency is to be expressed and brought out into the world. Finding these inbuilt qualities requires a cooperation with them instead of an individual struggle to create a more expressive life. In other words, the promise of our fulfillment is already 99% complete! The last percent is simply our allowing the expression to take place by means of our participation in a natural process. All we need to do is to look inside of our consciousness with intent and attention and invite our Genius to become expressive. Our attentive participation is the activating ingredient in this process of the integration of our Genius talents into our waking consciousness. Our work, then, is to remove the psychological barriers to this integration, first, by recognizing what the actual problem is, and then, by facing the demon (daimon) head on. It is at this point that we recognize that our devil is actually our own spirit that has been seen as something malevolent simply because it is always trying to disturb the existential sleep we have succumbed to, and to awaken us to greater insight and expression. It presents difficulties not to stop us from finding our Genius but in order to activate our stagnated creativity.

Imagine, for a second, that you are an orange tree. You have gone through the winter, and now springtime has arrived, and you have been busy soaking up water and nutrients from the ground. You have become full to the brim of your desired sustenance and are now ready to flower and bear the fruit that is uniquely yours to give outwardly to the world. Now imagine that every time you are ready to produce a flower, which is a portent of the orange to come, you have the habit of psychologically stopping it from budding. You have practiced this psychological habit for so long that it has now become so quick and automatic that it is unnoticeable, and the burden of all of the unborn fruit not given a chance to grow becomes a dull, existential ache that lingers on the fringe of your consciousness—there, but not recognizable as anything but a symptom of something being terribly wrong with you that you can't quite put your finger on. Now imagine, as this tree, turning your attention inward and finding that exact moment when you psychologically stop the budding of your flowers. Simply by turning your attention to this habit begins to change and dissolve it through the application of a nonjudgmental awareness to it. Without judgment, the habit is free to change of its own accord, and the natural flowering will take place.

Remember that our friend Aristotle's *eudaimonia* meant finding the best in ourselves and expressing it. For many of us in midlife, this expression may appear to others as an about-face or even an abandonment of a long-held belief system that no longer works for our current reality. Some may wonder what has happened to us to make us turn from our rational and logical approach to life to pursue a seemingly crazy and useless enterprise, which seems completely out of character for us. The real question at midlife is "Which character is more authentically me at this point?" This question can only be answered by each of us as individuals, and we need to be willing to undergo the requisite struggle to uncover our authentic identity as it exists in the here and now of our lives.

I lived for most of my adult life in a spiritual community whose members strove for the ideal of spiritual enlightenment. I would give bi-weekly discourses on the importance of dissolving individual consciousness into universal consciousness and about always returning to the light of God through meditation when the ego in us engages in thoughts of separateness. This ideal served me well for a great many years until our community broke up, and I lost my friends, spiritual family, vocation, and faith all at once. After many years of dark and confusing times, I have had to reverse and amend my positions on many tenets of that light-focused ideal. Most of those positions no longer fit or serve the new reality that has evolved through my dark times. It has been difficult to reconcile the person I had been before, as seen by others, with the person I am now as a result of my experiences. One thing that helped me make the transformation was the unique experience of suffering brought on by a long overdue course correction of my soul.

Suffering can bring the amazing gift of freedom from being concerned about how you appear to others. We suffer alone. No amount of explanation can convey the experience to someone else, and there is a great value to any uniquely personal test and transformation. In the solitude of suffering, a new version of a person is born who is more of an individual than the previous version had been. As I have said before, being an individual means to be one who is no longer divided within oneself. This personal unification of the opposites within brings the energy needed to make a successful midlife journey filled with discovery and fulfillment.

It follows then that one of the greatest perks of midlife, after having gone through many years of living through the expectations of others and the need to be seen in a positive light, is realizing that others' opinions about us really don't matter very much. We are free at this point, to put it bluntly, not to give a shit about others' ideas of us. Living the first half of life for the expectations of others can exhaust our energy to a point where, in order to survive as our genuine selves, we have to let go of our concerns about how we appear to others. Those who love us will love us; those who don't really don't factor at all into our happiness or fulfillment. Having a limited time left to live instead of having the youthful illusion of living forever changes our outlook about what is ultimately important. We are standing on a different hill now than someone younger, and from this unique vantage point, we can see how little others' opinions of us have actually mattered in the long run.

Using this midlife quality of decreasing the emphasis we've placed on what others think is an essential ingredient if we plan on following our Genius' path. Since there is no telling where it may lead, we need the freedom and energy we have gained from releasing our concern about others' ideas of us to make our unique journey. We need the buoyancy that comes from being unencumbered by others' expectations of us. We need to stop seeking others' permission to become our Genius selves.

Philosophy vs. Living

Midlife is an important time for our Genius to be lived, expressed, and cultivated. An idea that we can work with in terms of discovering Genius in midlife is *If not now, when?* In early adulthood, while we are actively creating the identities that are necessary for interfacing with our culture and society, we are usually once removed from our Genius qualities and their manifestation in our lives. Since our Genius is a part of our existential make up, and since it thrives on being brought to the forefront of our awareness, it can only go unexpressed for so long before it begins to complain to us in our bodies or psyches in the form of mysterious symptoms such as physical diseases, depression, or anxiety. Even though we may be making healthy life choices, or have what other people may see as a "perfect life" in terms of possessions and circumstances, if our Genius isn't happy and expressive, we will suffer from a deep feeling of discontent. Knowing, first of all, that we have a Genius spirit can help us to understand and relieve this suffering by allowing our Genius traits to come out and play.

Many people live their lives strictly as philosophers versus as practitioners. Its fine to have a well-developed personal philosophy of life and the universe, but if no personal actions emanate from our philosophy out of a felt sense of responsibility to "walk the talk," our philosophical insights remain in seed form. They do not sprout or bloom. If we don't risk putting our philosophies to practice in our lives by planting their seeds in the nutrient-rich soil of our experience, they will never take root or grow into something useful or provide anything vital and useful to the world. An unplanted seed is a genuine tragedy; nothing risked, nothing gained.

The 18th-century British author Samuel Johnson had a colleague and schoolmate named Oliver Edwards, who said to him one day, *"You are a philosopher, Dr. Johnson. I have tried too in my time to be a philosopher; but, I don't know how, cheerfulness was always breaking in."* Edwards seemed to me to be speaking of Genius vs. philosophy. When we are expressing and living our Genius way, we experience a sense of cheerfulness that doesn't come necessarily from the results of our efforts but rather from the expression of Genius itself. The reward of allowing our Genius to express is immediate, and cheerfulness can only exist in the present moment, not in retrospect or in the future. Edward's "cheerfulness breaking in" was happening in spite of his attempts to become a philosopher. He tried, but couldn't remain being a philosopher of unplanted seeds because it wasn't in harmony with his Genius, which always crashed his philosophy party in the form of cheerfulness.

Living our Genius way is different from merely accepting and agreeing with the idea of Genius. Living Genius means that risks have to be taken, old patterns have to be shaken off, and room for the unexpected has to be made every day. Genius will always challenge our status quo, preferring instead to spark something new in us that may be out of character but that may be just the thing that can save us from our stagnated philosophy.

There are times, as illustrated in the following story when action is needed; when stubbornly sticking to our philosophy keeps us trapped.

There was once a man, a grammar teacher, who was walking through some thick woods one day. While thinking about his next class, he inadvertently fell into an abandoned well. He broke his arm in the fall, and there was no way for him to climb out. He began to shout for help, and it wasn't long before someone heard him. A shepherd came running from a nearby field and shouted down into the well, "What is your situation?"

The grammar teacher replied, "I have broken my arm and can't climb out on my own. Can you help me?"

"Yes, I can," said the shepherd. "Give me a few minutes to go and fetch a rope."

The grammar teacher, out of sheer habit, said, "Wait a moment, please. The proper word to use is bring. *You should say, 'I will bring a rope.'"*

"Very well," the shepherd replied. "I was under the impression that the most important thing was pulling you up from that well. Instead, I'll take your advise and learn to speak correctly before I come back to save you. Good luck!"

The grammar teacher had lost perspective of his situation by habitually returning to his insistence on proper grammar. He forgot that he was stuck, without a way out. He failed to recognize the value of the shepherd who was there to save him.

If we can discern the most important thing to do, moment by moment, we can come to see that approaching a situation in a new way is far superior to our usual and habitual response. When we act, we risk. Risk of something new doesn't guarantee success, but it does guarantee results. A result of some sort always occurs when we dare to allow our Genius qualities to be put into motion. This result will always teach and inform us in some manner. We will find ourselves farther along on the Genius way. When we stubbornly cling to the old and outdated versions of ourselves, we miss out on the auspicious events that are designed to change us into something new and more congruent with the opportunities that exist in the here and now of our lives.

Libido and Genius

> "What is it, at this moment and
> in this individual, that represents the
> natural urge of life? That is the question."
> *— Carl Jung*

By the time many of us reach a midlife crossroads, which may manifest with such issues as health concerns, changing of jobs, marital problems, or a nagging question of life purpose, we probably will have noticed a drop in libido. Libido is the life force energy or natural urge and desire of life needed for us to move forward into the next chapter of our lives with enthusiasm and creativity. Without the access to a full-flowing libido, the task of stepping into a new psychological space or life expression will seem daunting if not impossible.

The Latin word *libido*, meaning "desire" or "lust," was used by Sigmund Freud in his theories to represent psychic energy, specifically the sexual energy of human beings as outlined in his theory of the psychosexual stages of development. As a consequence, *libido* is the term commonly used today when referring to the strength of a person's sexual drive. Freud also believed that only a limited amount of libido is available to each individual and that repression of certain emotions and tendencies can take up much of the libido's energy, leaving little left over for conscious use. Jung, who spent time in his early career as Freud's protégé, saw libido as having to do with more than sexuality. His understanding was that libido was an impulse or desire that remained unchecked by any type of authority. He saw it as the natural appetite of our life force for different levels of human experience and expression. Regarding the libido's qualities, he said, "The libido has, as it were, a natural penchant: it is like water, which must have a gradient if it is to flow."

> "A stagnant pool abides in peace. It is the peace of death. The living waters always skip and leap about like lambs in spring."
> — *Aquarian Gospel of Jesus the Christ*

That is to say that libido will move on its own, like water, where there is a gradient, slope, or pathway, and that the task of the individual is to create or allow a conducive channel for its flow. It takes an effort on our part to allow libido to flow effortlessly.

Just a quick note: Jung's departure from Freud's concept of libido was not convenient for him. It landed him in a state of contention with Freud, who had mentored him in his early career and had groomed him as the successor to his theories. However, Jung saw libido as he saw it, from his own world of genius insight. He chose to be true to his individual convictions, which led to a split with Freud and a confusing period of time for Jung, which included a psychotic break. He was willing to pay the price to be authentic and to be true to his Genius qualities.

Our Genius spirit is part of this natural life urge and has its own instinctual desire to express its unique qualities outwardly into the world. We can help to bring out this expression by paying attention to the messages that are consistently coming from our Genius spirit and by allowing ourselves to imagine again. Imagination can create the "gradient or slope" that Jung spoke about, which allows the water of our life force to move and flow again. It is essential to the Genius spirit to have this free movement of energy in order for it to become a part of our conscious life expression. If we can imagine, wonder, and become open and available to its desire for expression, we will be able to experience the happiness, freedom, and satisfaction that specifically comes from expressing our individual and unique Genius qualities.

A great question for those who feel that their vital life force has stagnated in midlife is:

> "How can I create the conditions to allow my *libido* life force to move and flow again?"

What we should realize is that even getting to a point in our lives where we can feel the stagnancy and ask the question is setting the stage for change. It has taken a great deal of unconscious effort applied to the repression of our natural Genius tendencies to stagnate a vital, boundless energy such as libido, whose primary quality, like water, is the provision of the energy that provides movement. Movement means that something different can actually happen, and something can definitively change. At midlife, most of us are ready for that change and are willing to do whatever it takes individually to facilitate a "slope" so that our water-like libido can move and thus change us.

If we take a look at the time period of our early adulthood up to the period of midlife, most of us can see that we spent a great deal of effort to keep things the same and to avoid change. Our careers, relationships, responsibility to family, building our identity, and our desire for security demanded that effort, as we fended off the threats that would endanger our physical and psychological securities. The problem with striving for security by trying to remain the same is that it goes against a basic principle of life itself. Life *is* change. Life *is* movement. It doesn't seem to care about what we consider important or our ideals of a perfect life situation. And sooner or later, if we don't move and change, life will do it for us. Remember that life is not simply happening to us; life *is* us. We are part of life's dance, and although we can engage in the practice of our free will, we should realize that free will is only a part of the equation. We have come to this life with unique Genius qualities that want to express themselves regardless of our ideas about who we are.

I have a Japanese-American friend whose parents were Japanese immigrants who never learned to speak a great deal of English or became enculturated into American society. My friend however, was born in the United States and grew up in a Southern California town as a full-blooded American girl, completely integrated into American culture. She remembers thinking until a certain age that she was actually a blonde-haired, blue-eyed person, just like many of her friends at school. One day in her early adolescence, she had a shocking experience as she looked in the mirror and actually saw a black-haired Japanese girl in the reflection. As convinced as she was that she was actually Caucasian, that day, a psychological fog simply lifted and revealed the fully formed expression of her Japanese DNA. Her physical features were there all along, just as our Genius features remain intact and unique in us.

My friend's experience is a metaphor of how someone's innate qualities can suddenly show up out of nowhere when least expected. People at midlife who feel the need for a change in their self-expression have no desire to wait around for something to change. Coming out of the adolescent illusion of invincibility and of living forever, we become aware of our limited amount of time left, and we feel the need to act. Becoming aware of our eventual death brings a motivation for growth like no other. We can consider it a midlife gift that appears in our awareness at the perfect time.

Picking up the idea of free will again, rather than utilizing our free will to force a desired change to happen, we can actually use it to create the circumstances for our life force to move and flow again, bringing our Genius qualities along for the ride. Our free will is how we can tune in and participate with life's movements by becoming sensitive and intuitive to their secrets. We create a slope for our libido to move along by approaching our stagnancy with curiosity, creativity, and imagination. This is the greatest work we can do to allow what is within us to manifest, remembering that the energy we are creating a path for is not circumscribed by our individual bodies or egos but rather carries the imprint and primal force of life itself.

Libido Exercise

Do this exercise in front of your computer or with a pen and paper. Read one line, close your eyes, and experience what happens in your imagination. Then write down what you experience. Then read the next line and repeat.

You have a small garden that is in desperate need of water. Your plants are drying up and there is no sign of rain in the immediate future. You decide to go in search of a source of water. Imagine walking up a grassy hill. You are carrying a shovel with you. On the top of the hill, you discover a small pond. You can see that the pond water is still and that someone has built a raised mound of dirt around its edges. Without anything moving into it or out from it, it has become stagnant and dead.

- Take note of the color of the water. Can you see into it or is it opaque?
- Is there anything growing in the pond? Flowers, water plants, algae?
- Do you notice anything living in the pond? Fish, turtles, snakes, snails?
- What kind of smell does the pond have?

- The pond has a voice. What does it say to you?

- You remember that where you live, down the hill, you are in need of water for your garden.

- What have you planted in your garden?

- What condition are your plants in?

- You begin to use your shovel to dig through the wall surrounding the pond to release the water.

- What do you discover in the dirt that you dig up?

- Is it easy or difficult to dig through the wall?

- Do you finally succeed in getting to the water? If not, what is in your way?

- If you do get through, you notice that the water begins to flow naturally downhill toward your garden.

- Does it trickle or run down in torrents?

- Has the quality of the water changed?

Take a few moments to witness any feelings or insights that arise from this experience. Write them down and realize that you can repeat this exercise as many times as you would like. This is an inner exercise of symbolically creating a slope for your life energy to move along and to become active in your life experience again. In this way, you can utilize the energy that has been stuck and misdirected to things that don't serve you anymore. When this life energy is allowed to move, it will take its natural path, reawakening your Genius traits and life purpose.

6

Chaos and Alchemy

One thing that the deep and urgent questions about life meaning and purpose appearing during midlife can do for us is to create the perfect conditions for new beginnings to occur. Enthusiasm, inspiration, vision, and creative energy all need rich and fertile ground from which to sprout and grow. In order for the ground of our consciousness to become fertile with potential, it first needs to be disturbed; something needs to turn it over, cracking the hard surface and exposing what was once underneath to the open air and sunlight. Things that we may have successfully hidden from ourselves and from others for a long time, including a deep dissatisfaction with the way our lives have been going, suddenly come to the surface and demand our attention.

Our conscious soil can be disturbed by a myriad of occurrences such as an illness, a breakup with a partner, or moving to a new area or changing jobs. Whatever the reason, our inner worlds are thrown into a state of chaos. Familiar patterns of thinking are disrupted, people that we used to count on for bearings and reference in our lives may no longer serve that purpose, and instead of having answers, we are thrown into a chaotic world of unending questions and doubts about who we are as a person and where we are heading.

This state may sound grim and unbearable, but we have to remember that in order to create a possibility for something new, something old has to go. Chaos can be seen as the spring cleaning of our consciousness, and things that we haven't used or haven't worked for a long time will have to be discarded to create the space needed for newness and potential. The chaos that is created from cleaning out our inner drawers, closets, and garages comes from the natural pendulum swing and course correction that life itself brings, and our only job is to keep ourselves from going out to the curb and retrieving the discarded junk that has been cluttering our inner hallways for far too long. Getting used to the idea that chaos is a good thing requires a certain amount of trust in the transformational process. For this we can look to the idea of alchemy.

Alchemy as a Metaphor

The concept of alchemy is a useful metaphor for our inner transformation. The basic supposition held by ancient alchemists was that one could take a base metal such as lead, place it in some kind of vessel or container, and through the application of certain transformative processes such as heat, cold, or liquefaction, transform it ultimately into gold. In psychological terms, the alchemical process is the transformation of unconscious psychic material into the conscious realm with the ultimate goal of creating the *philosopher's stone,* which is the final outcome of our purest and highest potential as human beings. The process always begins with what is known as *prima materia* or "primal matter." One simile for this primal matter is none other than chaos.

It is of little wonder that a term alchemists used to describe our primal chaos was the Latin term *massa confusa*:

massa meaning "mass, load, or burden of material" and *confusa* meaning "to be thrown into disorder; to trouble or disturb." What the alchemists knew was that chaos was a necessary and fortunate state. It contains the building blocks of any kind of transformation.

In order to use the chaos in our lives as a transformative vehicle, we will first have to recognize the life-changing potential that inner upheaval and chaos contain and, more importantly, learn to allow the change to happen instead of fighting it. We must learn to see our chaos as a friend who has taken our car keys after a night of drinking too much and interrupts our long-practiced tendency to drive home drunk. Or we can see chaos as a surgeon who recognizes that, to save our life she must first remove our ruptured appendix so that the toxins being released don't actually kill us. Instead of being anesthetized for this psychological operation, however, we are required to be conscious and awake the whole while. A problem arises when we think that we have to do something during this confusing time to "fix" what is wrong. Any time we experience something unpleasant, we naturally want it to stop hurting. We want to preserve the continued functioning of our lives as we have come to know them. What we have to realize about this period of chaos and transformation is that it is necessary but also temporary. It's like we're riding on a crowded bus when another passenger gets on, and we have to move a little bit to make room for him. Although it may be crowded and uncomfortable, we trust that things will sort themselves out and that we will make our way out of the crowd when we reach our stop. We know this because it happens all over the world, every day. We make some space, wait, and trust. We can also make space for the chaos and just stand there for a little while in a state of trust as things sort themselves out. We can't plan or control the ebb and flow of passengers on the bus any more than we can plan or control an inner transformation. We can just learn to let it happen. Nothing is going wrong; our ship is righting itself and correcting its course toward a promising future.

Finding a Container

Another vitally important element in alchemy is to use some sort of container into which we put our chaos or primal material in order to facilitate its transformation. One name for such a container is a *retort*. Picture a laboratory beaker or test tube that is used for experiments. Keeping the transformative properties contained safely in the retort allows the requisite processes of change to take place undisturbed. What is important here is for our primal matter to remain in the retort for the duration of the process and for us not to leave it if the heat gets turned up or some unfamiliar sensations begin to surface. In terms of psychological alchemical change and transformation, a retort can be a relationship such as one with a professional therapist, a mentor, friend, or partner who is aware and supportive of our transformation. A retort could also be a diary or journal, a blog, meditation practice, or prayer. What is important is that we use the container as a place to let go of the idea of controlling our transformation and to simply let the mysterious changes happen in spite of us. While we are in the safety of the retort, there is nothing to do but to let go and witness the process.

The role of Imagination in Accessing Genius

"Without this playing with fantasy no creative
work has ever yet come to birth. The debt we owe
to the play of the imagination is incalculable."
— *Carl Jung*

Everything we see around us made by man was originally a fantasy image in someone's mind. The fantasy was given the freedom to exist, morph, and change as much as it wanted, and it was not subject to the limitations of what was known or possible at that point in time. Imagination is solely responsible for pushing the boundaries of what was known.

I invite you to consider nature's creation as manifesting the same way. Beginning in the Universal mind as a fantasy, creation dreams and imagines something into existence, it seems, not necessarily for the sake of practicality but more for the fun of creation and exploration. It's as if something is saying "Why not this too? Let's see what happens." Look at a single flower without your scientific glasses for a moment, and you'll find no reason for that particular one appearing the way it does; look at the myriad of shapes, forms, and colorings of sea creatures on a coral reef; look at pictures taken by our space telescopes to see countless galaxies of star systems, each having their own shapes, forms, and colors. If you don't see this as proof of an immense imagination at work, then you are looking as an outsider and not with the insight of your innate Genius, who sees imagination as the seed of physical reality.

If we go one step further, we will see ourselves and our unique Genius traits as having been imagined into existence by something else. This something else, for the sake of this interpretation, can be called the *Universal mind*. This Universal mind has no limitations or boundaries to its imagination. Once it imagines one thing, like one human being complete with Genius qualities, it never repeats that same image again. What would be the fun in that? Each imagined human Genius is a potential form of a unique expression of the Universal mind that will only occur once in eternity; hence, the inherent urgency we feel, especially at midlife to allow this expression to take place. We finally are drawn to act upon our deeply felt responsibility to live out our gifts of uniqueness and give them to the world.

Like me with the creation of my handcrafted furniture, a fantasy image that was actualized by means of a certain knack I had with wood now has its own, autonomous life. For the most part, I have no idea where those pieces of furniture are now, how they are being used, or by whom. However, they will always carry my certain energy signature as their creator: a quality uniquely mine, expressed through my Genius, which, in turn, was expressed through the Universal mind.

Finding Your Genius Images

In order to locate our Genius, we need to look no further than our inner imaginal life, and to the qualities of our images that we have kept hidden from the world and others. They are a living potential in our unconscious and are seen as unreal only until given serious attention and consideration by us. Their potential is the key, because the energy they contain in potentiality, when released, has the power to manifest in our conscious lives. The foundation of any image is the natural impulse in us for the expression of something specific. This impulse is an energetic urge from our Genius that knows what it wants to express and that is quickly translated into imaginal language. Finding a way to speak our Genius's imaginal language is the key to its expression in our lives.

Active Imagination

Imagination is as intrinsic to our psychological makeup as muscle and blood are to our physical bodies. Our thoughts arise following the rise of images in our psyche, and these images are the language of the soul. They are our connection to the unconscious parts of us which can be encountered by turning our attention inward and acknowledging and dialoging with them.

Each of us can witness monologues and dialogues occurring simultaneously against the backdrop of our minds. There are always at least several voices talking in our heads at once, often to each other as the pro and con sides in a debate. Each has a distinct personality that has its own unique and important story to tell us. Usually, these conversations between the different characters in our unconscious are going on without our awareness. They are passive and thus unable to integrate or transmute their energy into something that becomes available to us for use in our outwardly facing lives. Without directing our conscious attention to them, these inner debaters behave in a chaotic and nonintegrated way. However, we can actively engage in conversations with these parts of our psyche as a practice and as a means to know, understand, and integrate them into a fuller sense of being and identity. The voice of our Genius is part of this cacophony of voices, and we can direct a conscious, active dialog with it. Imagination becomes active by bringing our consciousness to it, which differentiates it from mere daydreaming.

Talking to our Genius deliberately for the sake of self-discovery is not a sign of mental illness but rather a way to acknowledge the messages that it is sending to us. The information they carry can provide amazingly poignant insights and answers to problems and situations that have been difficult for us for a long time. Now, instead of ignoring what our Genius is saying and consequently feeling drained of creativity and inspiration, we are literally energized by the release of Genius contents into our conscious life.

Meditation vs. Active Imagination

The difference between meditation and active imagination is that the psychic material discarded by meditators as a worthless distraction instead is met with attention, honor, and engagement by practitioners of active imagination.

My particular history with the practice of self-discovery and looking inward for answers included my 30-year practice of Eastern-based meditation techniques, which, when practiced diligently, carry the promise of enabling one to achieve a state of enlightenment that transcends the conflicting voices of one's mind. Practitioners are advised not to give any credence to thoughts that arise but, instead, to cling to the transcendental light inside their consciousness whenever they find that their attention has wandered away with some "random" image or thought. Images and thoughts in this type of practice are seen as distractions to one's conscious awakening and connection to God, which promises the experience of bliss and joy. Anything unconscious is seen as undesirable, low, and even evil in its attempts to lure the meditator away from the transcendent light.

After the breakup of my spiritual community, I found that I could no longer engage in meditation practice in this way. It became viscerally repugnant to me. It was no longer serving me or helping to solve the internal problems that had arisen. Historically, my meditation practice had ignored my Genius qualities and their expression and dismissed them as "ego" or self-centeredness. For many years without realizing it, my experience had become rotten and stagnant from ignoring what was unique in me as an individual. In a very real way, my years of the practice of "going into the light" had set me up for a period of severe depression because of my inadvertent disregard and suppression of the messages being brought up by these "distracting images" from my Genius. My path to inner freedom actually became a beautiful trap that I had fallen into under the guise of my devotion to its practice. This practice did not include listening and trusting what my Genius spirit was communicating to me and what I, in particular, needed in order to evolve and individuate.

Luckily for us, Genius has a persistent quality, and will not let us rest in stagnancy. Regardless if we turn within and listen to it or not, it continues to send its messages into our lives in imaginative and creative ways. Its communication may appear as a moment of inspiration when we notice a glint of sunlight through a window, or it could easily manifest as a symptom of an illness, physical or psychological. Whatever the expression, it comes to awaken us to a greater potential that we are not yet living.

Regarding our personal daimon or Genius, Hillman says,

> Each life is formed by its unique image, an image that is the essence of that life and calls it to a destiny. As the force of fate, this image acts as a personal daimon [genius], an accompanying guide who remembers our calling. The daimon [genius] motivates. It protects. It invents and persists with stubborn fidelity. It resists compromising reasonableness and often forces deviance and oddity upon its keeper, especially when neglected or opposed.

Our Genius, then, is the thing that forever remembers and reminds us of our unique calling. We can consider ourselves extremely lucky to have ourselves "inconvenienced" in this way, being consistently disturbed by our Genius when we are ignoring what we have come here to do. Genius will never stop speaking to us in any way it can. Like water, it will flow through any tiny crack in our life template. It is our job to make the cracks bigger so that more Genius expression will shine through us and into the world.

Our inner psychic reality is filled with and communicates through images and symbols, so the language spoken there may be referred to as an imaginal language. We have come to know the word *imaginal* to mean an illusion, something that is not real. But for thousands of years, people who have studied and worked with human psychology have observed that, just as the outer physical world has its "realness," the inner world is no less real simply because its environment possesses different qualities than those of the outer world. We have an inner life that, although mostly unexplored, is nonetheless genuine and complete.

One way of encountering and inviting our Genius to have a role in our lives is through the practice of active imagination, in which we engage with our inner world consciously. It is designed to bring some of our unconscious content into conscious awareness, with the end result of gaining the energy and insight that this type of encounter can bring. Engaging in this practice can help to create a psychological integration that is deeply needed for an individual at midlife. Active imagination is not daydreaming. On the contrary, and in the case of dialoging with our Genius, we deliberately turn our attention inward to see what it has to say. We anticipate and expect a definite response. We are consciously awake for the entire process, and what takes place becomes part of our life experience.

The term *active imagination* was coined by Jung, who developed this technique, although shamans and healers throughout history have practiced it in one form or another. Jung used active imagination in his own personal psychological quest as well as with his psychotherapy clients. He stressed the need to approach its practice with a sense of respect for the messages emerging from our unconscious, as well as with a responsibility to integrate consciously the information it reveals into our life experience. Engaging in a dialog with our Genius qualities therefore should be taken seriously and with an intention to listen and *act* on the answers we receive.

Whenever we have an outward-facing experience, we're also having an inner one, where a reaction takes place in our inner consciousness simultaneously with an experience in our physical reality. This is what we are communicating when we say that "something has happened." If we have the experience of receiving an unexpected gift from someone, for example, we receive the external gift and simultaneously have an inner experience of surprise, gratitude, or some other inner response. When we practice active imagination, unconscious or repressed material enters our consciousness. Although the inner component actually occurs without the outer experience, it too can be seen as having "happened," because we consequently carry the memory and experience of it along with the insight that can be taken forward into future experiences. It is the same kind of insight that can be gained by having an experience in the outer world. Regarding active imagination, Jung said,

> Looking, psychologically, brings about the activation of the object; it is as if something were emanating from one's spiritual eye that evokes or activates the object of one's vision. The English verb "to look at" does not convey this meaning, but the German *betrachten*, which is an equivalent, means also to make pregnant. . . . And if it is pregnant, then something is due to come out of it; it is alive, it produces, it multiplies. That is the case with any fantasy image: one concentrates upon it, and then finds that one has great difficulty in keeping the thing quiet, it gets restless, it shifts, something is added, or it multiplies itself; one fills it with living power and it becomes pregnant.

Exercises in Finding Our Genius

The first thing to know about any exercise in self-observation and exploration is how the term *exercise* is being used. Commonly, this term indicates a movement or effort of some kind—in other words, *doing* something either physically or mentally in order to achieve a desired result.

In terms of the exercises in this book however, the word *exercise* is equated with a state of *being* rather than *doing*. Resting in a state of being allows us the time and space for an impartial observation of the information and psychological content that arises as a result of our inner explorations. This resting state serves as an impartial backdrop on which pictures, images, and feelings from our interiority appear. In a state of being rather than doing, we can bring a gentle and curious awareness to these images, and gain deep insights into important aspects of our inner workings.

> "Sitting silently, doing nothing, springtime comes and the grass grows all by itself."
> — *Matsuo Basho*

The exercises in the following pages all use some form of active imagination as their basis. As you begin to use these exercises to uncover and bring to light hidden aspects of yourself that will be valuable to your midlife transition, remember to approach each step with an open heart and mind, not judging what comes up in your experience, and simply taking note of the thoughts, feelings, and images as they arise spontaneously in your awareness.

Active Imagination Exercise

To begin with, one of the most effective ways in which we can encounter our Genius is by adopting an inner state of ease and of letting go rather than the idea of struggling alone up a steep mountain. Even if your Genius qualities happen to point you in the direction of mountain climbing, that predilection can be revealed by actively letting your Genius speak of its own volition.

Again, the technique of *active imagination* is a way of encountering and bringing unconscious psychic content that can be instrumental in clarifying and providing to our waking consciousness insights into our current situation.

This type of imagination is called *active* because we are deliberately turning our conscious attention to the images that arise as a result of our asking our unconscious to bring them up. It is important to realize that these images are coming from a part of us that most people largely ignore for most of their lives. The imaginal language that our unconscious speaks may seem foreign but, nonetheless, is coming from a uniquely personal realm that is as much a part of us as our outward facing personality.

A common notion for novice practitioners of active imagination is that they are just "making things up" when images arise to the level of their conscious awareness and that it is all just useless daydreaming and fantasy. Keep in mind that while some critical part of yourself may doubt that these seemingly random images are a personal and unique response to your question, it happens that *these* images in particular are appearing in your consciousness in *this* particular way, as opposed to the uncountable alternative images that could appear in the realm of possibility. As you follow the exercise outlined below, it is therefore crucial to take these images seriously, with a spirit of gentle curiosity for the fact that they are appearing to your conscious self.

- Sit in a comfortable position, back straight, feet on the floor, and close your eyes.

- Take a deep breath and exhale, making a space inside yourself for your exploration to take place.

- Inwardly ask the question 'What are my genius qualities?"

- Take note of any images or words that spontaneously arise, without judgment or critique.

- Write these images or words down, or record them as you go, noting any feelings or emotions accompanying them.

- Continue to have a dialog with this image or character for as long as you wish, keeping a non-critical, simple awareness of what takes place.

- Write down your questions and the responses that you receive.

- Remember to engage with the image, character, or feeling as you would communicate to another person.

- Ask your questions, respond with your genuine feelings about the information you receive. Most importantly, be yourself in this exchange.

- In this way, you will be integrating the psychic energy coming from the unconscious into your conscious persona by having an experience of participation with rather than a lecture from a deeper part of yourself.

- When you are ready, gently acknowledge the exchange that took place, take a deep breath, and slowly open your eyes.

Exercise on Being

- Sit in a comfortable position, back straight, feet on the floor, and close your eyes. Now, take in a deep breath and exhale, making a space inside yourself for your exploration to take place.

- As you sit quietly, become aware of the physical sensations your body is experiencing. Feel the temperature of the air on your skin, the different pressures on the places where your body is touching your chair, the feeling of your feet firmly on the floor.

- Now simply observe your heartbeat, sensing the unseen energy that sustains its functioning.

- Become aware of your breath, moving effortlessly in and out of your lungs all by itself. Tune in to the silent consciousness that gives the impulse that expands and contracts your lungs.

- Observe random thoughts and feelings that come and go. Don't try to stop them; let them move across the sky of your consciousness like lazy clouds drifting by on their own. Resting in this calm state of being, you have no need to apply any comments or judgments to your experience. You allow it to be simply what it is.

- Realize that this restful state of being is always present and available to you. This place is always at the foundation of whatever you happen to be doing. In fact, without being, there could be no doing.

Experience Inventories

Midlife is an excellent place in your life's path to take stock of where you've been and what you've actually accomplished along the way. Regardless of whether you consider your outward life as a success, as a failure, or a mix of both, it is important at this point to stop and rest on the side of the road and remember how you got to where you are now.

It is often helpful to write down what you discover while you are recalling your life experiences in order to compare them to the things that you decide you want to experience down the road in the future. The following three inventories focus on stages of your life. Answering the questions will provide a rough sketch of your Genius life map up until now.

Instructions

Sit down with your computer or a pen and paper available in order to document what arises in your consciousness during these exercises. Then read one question at a time, close your eyes and take a deep breath. On the exhale, see yourself making an inner space for your responses to the question to appear. You will have certain thoughts, feelings, images, or emotions arise in your awareness. Carefully and without judgment, allow them to appear just as they are without trying to change or understand them. When you have given them a chance to reverberate in your awareness for a short while, open your eyes and write down what you just experienced. Then move on to the next question. Remember that there are no right or wrong answers. Anything that comes to you is important information specifically coming from your inner identity.

Childhood Inventory

During early childhood, we have no other choice but to trust grown ups to help us bring out our Genius qualities. Some of us had help with this to some extent or the other, and some part of our Genius spirit was able to be expressed as a result, and our experimentations were encouraged and supported. Others grew up in situations where, perhaps out of necessity, Genius was never allowed to emerge, and others' ambitions and values were imposed on us before we could express our uniquely creative Genius impulses. Others' early life experiences were a combination of the two or were influenced by mixed messages sent by our caregivers about the importance of the expression of our young talents and qualities.

- What were some of your earliest memories of what you wanted to be when you grew up?
- At that time, in which ways did you express your creativity?
- How were you supported or discouraged in your expression?
- Was there a person or persons who contributed to the support or discouragement?
- Was there a grownup that you wanted to emulate? Which of their qualities attracted you?

Adolescence Inventory

Adolescence is a liminal space, a time between two identities, the child and the young adult, and can be one of the most confusing periods of a person's life. Adolescents feel a constant struggle and mounting pressure to create a unique identity which is separate from their identity as a child. Some aspects of childhood experience may evoke a sense of shame in adolescents for being so "naive and immature." Often the Genius qualities expressed in childhood don't survive the transition into adolescence and are abandoned along with other dreams and possibilities that, to the adolescent, no longer seem feasible due to the oncoming requisite identification with adulthood. So many amazing expressions that came directly from the Genius spark during childhood are abandoned at this stage, making way for expressions more readily accepted and expected by peers and an unenlightened society in which adolescents find themselves.

- What dreams and expressions were left off when you reached adolescence?

- Which Genius impulses were able to survive during this transition?

- Were there any new expressions of Genius uncovered during your adolescent years?

- What ideas and ideals did you get from others and embrace as your own?

- What habits did you develop during this period that remain with you to this day?

Young Adulthood Inventory

By this time, a solid ego identity has been formed, which may or may not be expressive of our Genius. We begin searching for the adult identity that is supposed to carry us all the way to the end of our lives. For anyone who was able to uncover and retain his or her Genius up until this point, life includes a creative outlet for its expression. However, this period can also become a path *away* from our Genius, depending on the experiences and ideas about life we've gleaned from our childhood and adolescence.

- What main ideal did you embrace about what it meant to be an adult?

- Which, if any aspirations, hopes or dreams did you abandon in order to try and live this ideal?

- Who was the main person or people who inspired you during this phase of your life?

- What habits did you form during this time period that have stayed with you to this day?

- Are these habits, routines, or ideals still serving who you want to be today?

You now should have some information regarding your genius's unique qualities. Take some time to consider which of these unique features if any have already manifested in your life, and if not, then what has happened to stop them from their outward expression.

7

Not Just for Children

Consider that at childhood, we are living very close to our genius qualities of vibrancy, creativity, and enthusiasm. Even children growing up in extremely difficult physical and psychological environments may still engage in play. It is not just the children's state of naïveté and innocence that allows this experience but also the proximity, availability, and expression of their individual Genius.

Over time, many of us unwittingly consigned our energy-giving Genius to our childhood memories and, as we grew into adults, became part of a larger society and accepted others' values and ideas about who we should want to be. We should realize however, that the amount of energy and enthusiasm and inspiration inherent in our Genius spirit is still just as available to us at any point in our lives if we make the attempt to uncover and reclaim it as a part of us. We will realize that childlike enthusiasm and joy is actually a lifelong quality that exudes from living our Genius. We actually can never lose it, but it may need to be recovered from the place we last left it. This uncovering is an adventure, ordeal, and quest that we embark upon when we realize that our Genius expression has been absent in our lives for far too long.

The Difference Between
Childlike and *Childish*

It is important here to distinguish the difference between being *childlike* and *childish*. *Childishness* is the tendency to act selfishly with an infantile set of behaviors belonging to children, who necessarily need to go through the developmental stage of creating a healthy ego, complete with the establishment of appropriate personal boundaries. In this state, children are not concerned with anything other than themselves, which is psychologically healthy and normal in terms of childhood development.

Being *childlike* is not a developmental stage at all but rather a state of awareness connected to soul and to the Genius spirit, which explores, creates, wonders, and imagines. Childishness is a state of development reinforced by saying "no," whereas being childlike is always an imaginative exploration and is reinforced by saying "yes."

When adults engage in childish behavior, they are exhibiting parts of themselves that remain stuck in an early developmental stage that was meant to create a healthy and separate sense of self by basically saying "no" to others. We can witness children going through this stage in their "terrible twos," when requests and instructions from parents are met with a negative response from their child at every turn. Although this is healthy behavior when we are 2 years old, as adults this kind of psychological "stuckness" will need to be worked through consciously and integrated into our adult identities in order to express the more universal and mature sense of being childlike.

Being childlike as an adult is to embody the Genius spirit of being open to new experiences and creating and imagining. The good thing about being childlike as adults is that, having a wealth of life experience to draw upon, we are no longer naïve and vulnerable to others' opinions of us. When we distill our experience into wisdom, we understand that those who truly love and accept us will allow us the freedom and space to reinvent ourselves whenever we feel the need to. We will also realize that being childlike instead of childish allows the expression of our Genius qualities, which carry an intrinsic sense of meaning and purpose.

Looking for Inspiration

I had taken a trip to Greece with my wife during my period of midlife existential angst, and I was looking to be inspired by the depth and wisdom of the ancient Grecian culture. We visited many beautiful islands and explored historically significant archeological sites and museums. All the while, I was asking for something. I couldn't quite put my finger on it, but I was searching for something that was missing from my life experience at the time. As our trip was drawing to a close, we were buying some gifts for family and friends when I saw some bracelets in a display case. They were made from braided string and silver beads etched with rustic symbols. I was drawn to one symbol in particular. It looked like a child's drawing of the sun—a small circle with lines representing rays emanating from it. All I can say is that it looked joyful to me, and I desperately needed some of that. It was explained to me by the shopkeeper that the symbol meant optimism. *Optimism* comes from the Latin word *optimum* meaning "best" and includes the word *ops*, which translates as "power or resources." Being naturally drawn at that time to a symbol for "the best power or resources" signaled that I was in need of a deep reconnection to my Genius and its energy-giving qualities, and something in me knew it.

Although, as adults, we unwittingly moved away from our energy-giving Genius, the childlike enthusiasm and joy we knew as children can be reclaimed as part of us. It's like rubbing the dust off of an old lamp and releasing the genie (Genius) within us again. We haven't lost it, we've just let the genius lamp get dusty from years of neglect and nonuse.

Notably, another manifestation of the Latin word *Genius* is *genie*, which is the French spelling of the Arabic word *jinni* used in the French translation of the *Arabian Nights* stories. Like Genius, a genie is defined as a teaching spirit. In one story in that collection, the genie has been imprisoned in a bottle and is released by a fisherman, who, in turn, experiences many interesting adventures and receives various rewards and boons. The phrase "letting the genie out of the bottle" commonly translates as a potentially dangerous enterprise that may have irreversible and uncontrollable consequences. Although the releasing of our Genius may challenge the status quo of our adult lives and seem dangerous to our deeply entrenched identities, by midlife we may actually feel that *not* to release our Genius is even more dangerous to our genuine selves.

Letting our Genius emerge from exile will allow new iterations of our original expression of our Genius in childhood to emerge and take shape. We may engage in creative endeavors and adventures that seem to others to be "out of character" for us. But if we're not willing by midlife to take a chance and express our innate Genius qualities out of a need to retain a consistent outward appearance in the eyes of others, we're not yet ready to do the course correction that is necessary to bring a change in the waking consciousness of our lives. With this reluctance, we may be depriving the world and those around us of the gifts we came to share.

The Importance of Play

"To stimulate creativity one must develop childlike inclination for play and the childlike desire for recognition."
— *Albert Einstein*

One thing that occurs for most of us by the time midlife rolls around is that we have stopped playing. Through our early adulthoods, we most likely have lived our lives in work mode in order to build a life for ourselves and our families. In the name of being a responsible adult, we strove to establish some kind of financial foundation and living situation. Unless we are athletes, musicians, or artists by profession, playing has been left in our pasts and exists as a memory of our irreplaceable childhood experience. In childhood, our instinct was to play just for the sake of playing, as it provided the exploration and experimentation necessary for growth.

The thing about play is that it's not just for children. There is an actual need for playing and experimentation that exists in us throughout our lives. Through play, we can be free to create and discover things that never could have been uncovered through any amount of dry thinking and arid reasoning. Closing off doors of exploration because they may seem silly or childish makes us old and out of touch with our Genius spirit. We actually need to play in order to rediscover our perennially creative natures. Again, this is a need, not an elective. Like food and air, our souls are fed by looking into unencumbered possibilities that we allow ourselves the freedom to explore beyond logic and reason. Creative play is the sustenance that feeds that part of us. Jung writes about the necessity of play:

> Every good idea and all creative work are the offspring of the imagination, and have their source in what one is pleased to call infantile fantasy. Not the artist alone, but every creative individual whatsoever owes all that is greatest in his life to fantasy. The dynamic principle of fantasy is play, a characteristic also of the child, and as such it appears inconsistent with the principle of serious work.

An underappreciated quality of play is that it can seem purposeless. We can play for no reason at all and become all the richer for it. Play is one thing that we can do for its own sake and nothing more. We don't have to justify it to anyone, because it's not done for anyone else's approval. We play simply because we feel like it. Adults have largely ignored this impulse out of the need to be accountable to their families and jobs for how they spend their limited amount of time. In that model, time needs to be turned into profit of some kind in order to justify one's existence. Play on the other hand needs no justification. Play's value, by definition, is the joy it can bring us. Approaching play in this way brings a requisite lightness to our hearts and souls that can resurrect the eternal childlike state of curiosity and wonder.

> "Play so that you may be serious."
> — *Anachrasis*

Numerous studies have been conducted on play and the effects it has on our wellbeing. When we engage in play for its own sake, the benefits include

- increased vitality and energy
- enhancement of relationships and intimacy
- a boost to our immune systems
- a felt sense of optimism and enthusiasm

Some of the consequences of not playing in our later lives are

- a greater risk of mental disorders
- increased risk of stress-related diseases
- higher instances of addictive behavior
- a greater risk of interpersonal violence

In other words, our human experience throughout our entire lifespan can greatly benefit from play and, conversely, suffer from the lack of it.

A paradox that exists concerning play in adulthood is that we have to accept play as an important responsibility. To do so, we need to redefine being "responsible" as an adult as having "the ability to respond." The trials that can be encountered at midlife require this ability as well as a psychological agility that can be accessed through a creative response to a challenging situation. Play is the source of that creative response. In order to engage in play, especially as midlife-aged adults, we have to be willing to appear silly or foolish and possibly be seen as a person who is wasting time. Armed with our life experience concerning what has ultimately and genuinely mattered, we realize that the potential of appearing foolish or being judged by others even while attempting to solve a problem in a rational or socially acceptable way is always a possibility. We have seen that there will always be antagonistic elements in our lives, and there will always be those who won't understand us. We have learned that the only way to approach happiness is by being true to ourselves regardless of others' opinions.

Our Genius can always be found in creative play. Simply listening to our Genius impulses can point us in the right direction for this kind of rewarding expression. Remember that Genius doesn't operate by reason or logic. To follow the trail of Genius, we have to be willing to trust that voice inside of us that is calling. Spontaneity is the hallmark of following our Genius, and there is no greater way to practice spontaneity than in play.

People have accomplished amazingly creative endeavors for a singularly simple reason: They weren't aware that their project couldn't be done. That is to say, they allowed themselves to play with the inspiration they received from their Genius spirit and treated their play and imagination with seriousness and determination, as if it were something that mattered greatly and needed to happen. They didn't become distracted by the stories of others' failures to accomplish similar things but chose instead to approach an imaginative idea with the sense of unique freshness available through the connection with Genius. David Campbell writes, "When truly creative people come up with a new idea they don't reject it immediately because of its flaws. They play with it, looking for strengths and sliding over weaknesses."

Playing allows for the growth of all things it touches. Ideas, skills, creativity, and our self awareness and understanding are accelerated and placed in high relief. How we approach play depends on how much we are willing to see through the eyes of our Genius qualities, which will always move like water through difficult situations to find a space to emerge. Looking with the eyes of our Genius changes our perception of events, as in this story:

> *One day, a teacher and his students were making their way through a small village. They walked past a heap of garbage and trash where someone had thrown the body of a dead dog. The students were expressing revulsion and disgust at the grotesque features and stench of the dog's rotting corpse as they walked by. The teacher, seeing the sunlight shining on the carcass remarked: "Look at how white that dog's teeth are!"*

Looking more deeply into this story, is this a matter of the teacher simply choosing to be positive? Is he merely being a contrary to his students? There may be another explanation for his response to this experience: He may be seeing creatively and playfully. He may be seeing through the eyes of his Genius that doesn't deny that there will always be ugliness in the world but gravitates to the beauty that exists regardless of that fact.

I recently had the experience of going to the DMV in order to register my car. A visit to the DMV is notoriously a long and tedious ordeal, and my experience was no exception. I waited for 3 hours and 20 minutes before my number was called, only to find that I didn't have the requisite supporting documents to register my car and that I would have to come back and repeat the same procedure. One of my personality traits is that I abhor having to do things twice. Once I'm done, I'm done, and I like to move on to the next thing. I felt a sense of anger at myself for not doing sufficient research and due diligence as well as a general annoyance at the seemingly mandated robotic nature of bureaucratic employees' behavior. As I walked outside in my indignant state, the sun was shining, and I could see the beautiful outline of a mountain and hills in the distance from the parking lot. I was filled with the realization that while I had "wasted" my day waiting for something that never happened, here I now was, in the sunlight, surrounded by great beauty. I had no more time to waste feeling angry. And life was good.

We can always find reasons for not allowing ourselves to play, but when play is seen as a lifeline to Genius and to our sense of fulfillment, we allow time for it in spite of our reasons and excuses not to.

Playing as an Adult

We can look to ourselves as children for clues about our Genius path. If we can experientially recall the realm of our unique and individual style of playing, we can reclaim the thread of imagination that still exists in us as adults. The key is to be able to suspend the accumulated experiences that define us as being middle aged by engaging our eternal child self in imaginative and spontaneous play. By following our guiding Genius spirit, we will be able once again to engage in spontaneous play for its own sake. This activity, in turn, can rekindle our living Genius qualities that we are here to manifest and express into the world.

Valid questions may arise about adult play, such as "How do I engage in play at this point of my life without abandoning my adult responsibilities? What will others think of me if I suddenly break into a spontaneous song or dance? What value can playing at this point in my life possibly have? How do I know if I'm doing it right?" Playing as an adult means to reencounter our innocence, and to see this active engagement with our innate imagination as a necessary and integral part of our entire human experience. Oddly enough, making space for spontaneous play needs to be taken seriously if it is to have an effect on our consciousness. To clarify this idea, these basic adult questions about play can be addressed.

How do I engage in play at this point of my life without abandoning my adult responsibilities?

We will need to reimagine ourselves as individuals who can connect to the storehouse of inspiration and possibility through creative play. What is being an adult? Many of us at midlife are asking this very important existential question at this point. If we can include the necessity of engaging in creative play as meeting an adult responsibility to remain vital and genuine, then the rewards of Genius play will appear in our daily lives and dealings with others.

What will others think of me if I suddenly break into a spontaneous song or dance?

We don't need to stop everything we're doing, say, in the middle of a workday, to engage in creative playing. It is not a requirement to follow every daydream and to express it outwardly. Genius play can be a private practice, like prayer or meditation; it is not meant as a public display of our spontaneity but as a deeply personal and healing activity.

What value can playing at this point in my life possibly have?

The value of play is that it emanates from our innate Genius and can help us to live more genuine lives by engaging with our imaginative spirit once again. Playing is not meant to stop because we've physically aged or because we've needed to become practical adults. Abandoning our capacity to play and to be creative puts us out of step with our deeper life, where Genius resides. We can actually come back to life by allowing ourselves the freedom to do something just for the sake of doing it, without any expectation for results and for the sheer joy of living spontaneously in the moment.

How do I know if I'm doing it right?

The best part of Genius play is that we can't do it wrongly. It is an expression of our uniqueness at the Genius level. Suspending our judgment of whether our play is being effective in bringing out our Genius will allow us simply to follow the breadcrumbs left for us on its path and see where our play leads. Play doesn't have to be any particular activity. It is simply an exercise in being naturally human without needing to explain or provide a reason for playing in our unique way.

A story often told about Jung refers to a time in his life when he was experiencing an existential crisis of identity. Somehow, he sensed that reencountering a point in his childhood through creativity and play would make available to him much-needed innate libido energy that could be used to help him navigate this difficult time in his life.

Beside the lake where Jung lived, he began to spend time every day stacking stones to create a miniature village of houses and castles. At the time, he didn't know what he was doing. He recalled, "I had no answer to my question, only the inner certainty that I was on the way to discovering my own myth. For the building game was only a beginning."

By his own description, during this time Jung had, in a way, gone mad. His conceptual world as it had been had crashed around his feet, and he was struggling to give this madness an expression in an attempt at healing himself. Eventually, he was able to attest to the value in such madness in this advice for others:

> Let the light of your madness shine, and it will suddenly dawn on you. Madness is not to be

despised and not to be feared, but instead you should give it life. . . . If you want to find paths, you should also not spurn madness, since it makes up such a great part of your nature. . . . Be glad that you can recognize it, for you will thus avoid becoming its victim. Madness is a special form of the spirit and clings to all teachings and philosophies, but even more to daily life, since life itself is full of craziness and at bottom utterly illogical. Man strives toward reason only so that he can make rules for himself. Life itself has no rules. That is its mystery and its unknown law. What you call knowledge is an attempt to impose something comprehensible on life.

The point about play, which may seem like madness at midlife, is that it doesn't need to be logical or even comprehensible. It doesn't follow any rules. The only requirement is that we allow it to happen as part of our Genius expression, and then accept what happens without judgment or expectation. We create and express something simply for its own sake.

Some suggestions to jumpstart your Genius play:

- Find a song whose words, melody, or message speaks to you, and sing it. This is not to be done as a performance or karaoke but instead a simple and spontaneous expression that you can feel as a physical vibration in your body. It can stop the rational mind in its tracks and place us in a timeless *kairos* state of being.

- Draw or paint an image from one of your dreams. When you wake up from sleep and have a dream that is still fresh in your consciousness, choose the most memorable image from the dream and draw it on paper.

Regardless of your skills as an artist, give shape and form to the image that has appeared to you, and go back later to look at it and let it resonate in your awareness without interpretation.

- Write a journal entry of one of your experiences. When you are moved in some way, positively, negatively, or indifferently, describe how you experience it by writing. Again, it is not necessary to write for the enjoyment of others but rather as a means of allowing the outer expression of your inner images that appear in revisiting your experiences.

All of these channels of expression accomplish a common thing: bringing our inner worlds into sharper focus by pulling our inner experience over the line into our outer lives. We are mining our inner Genius gold that has been waiting to be discovered and brought to the surface into our waking consciousness. There is nothing more satisfying, fulfilling, and healing than to give expression to an intrinsic part of ourselves that has been longing to be freed into consciousness.

Play, Ritual, and Rite

Hillman, with his archetypal perspective, takes the importance of play a step further into the realm of the divine. He expressed the importance of honoring imagination and play through various forms of consistent inner and outer acknowledgment of it by the individual:

The great task of a life sustaining culture, then, is to keep the invisibles attached, the gods smiling and pleased; to invite them to remain by propitiations and rituals; by singing and dancing, smudging and chanting; by anniversaries and remembrances; by great doctrines such as the Incarnation and little intuitive gestures — such as touching wood or by fingering beads, a rabbit's foot, a shark's tooth; or by putting a mezuzah on the door-post, dice on the dashboard; or by quietly laying a flower on a polished stone.

Ritual, in this case, doesn't allude to a dry practice or repetition of certain actions or static prayers but instead to an active acknowledgement of another living thing that is invisible to the outer world. Participating in life is the key to remaining in a creative flow, and acknowledging that there are unseen elements to our lives that support and inspire our creativity, expression, and our life's purpose and meaning creates a complete circuit of awareness of which we are a part. As modern humans, we have largely lost this concept of acknowledging the source of our inner strengths; consequently, we must look to cultures that still practice this daily recognition of the invisible forces actively working in our lives and on our behalf.

A story in the *Aquarian Gospel of Jesus the Christ* illustrates the necessity of acknowledging the gifts we are given that we have done nothing outwardly to deserve. The story emphasizes the importance of consciously turning toward this invisible thing, acknowledging it and saying thank you in some way, and indicates the great rewards received by participating in the universal and creative process of our individual evolution and development:

> *Jesus, all alone, went to the feast by the Samaria way; and as he went through Sychar on the way, the lepers saw him and a company of ten called from afar and said, "Lord Jesus, stay and speak the Word for us that we may be made clean. And Jesus said, "Go forth and show yourselves unto the priests." They went, and as they went their leprosy was healed. One of the ten, a native of Samaria, returned to thank the master and to praise the Lord. And Jesus said to him, "Lo, ten were cleansed;*

*where are the nine? Arise and go your way; your faith
has made you whole. You have revealed your heart and
shown that you are worthy of the power; behold the nine
will find again their leprous hands and feet."*

Rather than seeing this parable as a warning against
those nine who didn't acknowledge Jesus, or "the invisibles,"
as Hillman puts it, it can be viewed as a story about the part
of us that gets it: the part that intrinsically understands and
recognizes something at work on our behalf, clearing the
way for our continued development and healing. A requisite
part of that equation is our conscious acknowledgement that
such a thing is actually happening. This makes the process a
part of us. We are therefore acknowledging our own deeper
being and the processes that are constantly at play in support
of the development of meaning and life purpose.

Deliberately and naturally engaging in creative play can
thus be a form of the ritual of conscious acknowledgement of
our greater yet "invisible" selves and a rite of inclusion of
their unseen presence in our daily lives. Seen this way, play
is a holistic and existential endeavor that is the manifestation
of our deeper recognition of life's fundamental dynamics.
This ritual has an effect on us like none other, because in this
way, we are aware that we are indeed more than we appear
to be and have more energy at our disposal to express and
create the things that come natural to us.

Working With Our Hands

A particularly challenging aspect at midlife is to remain
creative and to learn to move through seeming impasses that
block the flow of our Genius qualities and our unique styles
of expression.

One way to kickstart our creative flow is to move from
our heads to our hands — in other words, to use our physical
bodies in a creative project involving anything from dancing

to painting, from building with wood to making clay figurines, or from planting a garden to fixing a car engine. The idea is to use all parts of ourselves including our bodies to restimulate our natural Genius creativity and allow its expression.

If we have been out of the practice of creative play for a while, perhaps even since childhood, it may take some time to learn to trust that our midlife phases of disorientation and confusion are actually pregnant with opportunity for creative expression. The dark nights of questioning the meaning of our lives and the periods of having no idea of our life purpose can be used to explore those very soul-based questions. We can see these situations as a creative challenge to grow and discover instead of simply falling into a state of physical and psychological inertia. Remember that movement and flow is the deep nature of the entire spectrum of our life experience. Our suffering comes from this flow being blocked in some way, either by self-imposed limitations on our fertile imagination or due to an unwillingness to allow our old ideas about ourselves to naturally drop off or change by the lessons of experience.

Turning to physical expression by using our hands to create something can free our minds from being focused on the seemingly insurmountable existential dilemma we are facing. By taking that problem to the bare ground of our physical existence, we are actively reaching for and calling on our primordial roots as human beings. We work with the mud and clay of our foundations to reboot our Genius traits that have been looking for a genuine and organic manifestation.

We can use the confusing times of midlife, ripe with its burning questions about our basic identities, as the impetus to move forward and through creative blocks and psychological brick walls. The murky and uneasy feelings that seep into our consciousness are actually the callings of our soul and Genius wanting to be rediscovered, honored, and given expression. When we forget this inner reality, we attempt to address these symptoms in a purely psychological way and ignore the role our physicality can play in their resolution and incorporation into our life experience.

A personal example that illustrates this practice is my own way of dealing with a writing block while I was writing about this very topic. I decided to turn to a physical expression of something in order to work through my creative impasse. My project was a backyard gazebo that I would build out of redwood lumber. After making plans and preparations for the structure, I began to work. Because the lumber I was using was very heavy, the first thing I had to do was to use my body to move each piece into place. I designed the gazebo with specific support joints, but I soon discovered that I lacked certain tools needed to create them. Many trips to the hardware store ensued. All the while, I was using my creativity and physicality to address the "problems" that arose.

An unexpected turn of events then called on my creativity in a different way. My neighbor, whose house sits on a small hill above mine, became upset upon seeing my project, because it took away a small portion of his view of the mountains that he was used to having all to himself. He yelled down the hill, called me an asshole, and promptly called the city building department to report me. My project that was designed for me to work with my hands had now become a legal issue, which threatened to derail my plans. Seeing this instead as an opportunity, I drew up city-approved plans, and after four trips to the building department, acquired an approved permit. This delay actually helped me to redesign the gazebo to a more suitable form, and I began construction again. At this point, my physical expression was even dearer to me because of all of the hurdles and blocks that I'd had to navigate in order to create it. Instead of rushing to complete the project, I noticed that I was taking my time and paying closer attention to the pure and spontaneous physical movements in which I was engaging: lifting, sawing, drilling, and painting. I liken this project to bypass surgery: being physically creative had removed a blockage to the heart of my Genius callings. The fresh blood of inspiration was able to flow again, and I experienced a surge of creative ideas to incorporate into the chapters of this book that I would never have received had I not gone through the building and permitting process. Thank you, gazebo. Thank you, neighbor. Thank you, city hall.

Creative Aging

When many of us think of our own aging process, we immediately conjure a negative association: a sense of deep loss as our youth fades. This loss, when seen through the lens of our young adult self, may also carry with it a sense of shame in being no longer who we once were. Things that we took for granted such as our physical strength and flexibility begin to wane. Lines appear on our faces; our hair begins to grey and thin. Through this shame lens, we can only see what is leaving us, and we feel a sense of betrayal at this process happening too soon. We aren't ready to die yet.

Many of us take the road of denial when we become aware of this process happening to us. Denial takes a great deal of our vital energy to maintain; hair dyes and skin treatments, sports cars and romantic affairs; anything to stave off the inevitable surrender to the slowing down of our physical functioning. In the process of denying our aging, we may also find ourselves carrying a sense of failure at not being able to remain as we once were. We usually don't think about the second half of life in terms of growth and evolution but rather as an indignity that has to be suffered. We are exposed now to all who can see our wrinkles and graying hair. Because we can no longer cling to the youthful illusion of immortality, we are now more aware of our vulnerability.

If we look closely, the reason for our feelings of shame, loss, or failure during the aging process is that something else from within us is telling us that there is more life to be experienced, but we aren't clear on how this is to come about. Something at our core remains youthful, still curious, adventurous, and enthusiastic, yet our physicality is painting a different picture altogether. Which messages do we listen to?

This is a time to engage in a more expanded way thinking that is inclusive of opposing truths we may find in every situation. We can say, "Yes, my body is showing signs of aging, and yet I also feel that I have much more to do and experience." We can feel unfamiliar aches, pains, and stiffness while also feeling the freedom of not having to repeat many painful life lessons because we have already learned them by experience. We can feel new physical limitations in movement while feeling inspired by a new idea or project. The fact is that we have more room now inside of us, our experiences having carved out a larger psychological space that can contain and hold both the desirable and undesirable as equal qualities of the human experience. In a nutshell, we have paid dearly to be where we are today, and we should take advantage of what we have gleaned from our lives along the way. The following exercise is a way of looking back along that path.

Looking Back Exercise

- Take a moment to feel like the age that you are now, whatever that feels like. Notice the different body sensations that you experience, thought patterns, and general complaints about life that you indulge in regularly.

- Now take a look back in time to a point in your youth. See yourself in a picture from that time and notice how young you look.

- Consider your dreams of the future at that time and all of the possibilities that lay before this younger version of yourself.

- As your older self, talk to this person about the problems and concerns they currently face, and add any insight about those things that you have gained from living through them.

- Were the problems of that time as large and consequential as you thought they were?

- In hindsight, should you have spent as much time as you did being concerned or worried about them?

- Now take a mental picture or snapshot of yourself in the present, at midlife.

- Look at it, notice what you see, and briefly describe yourself and your problems and concerns.

- Project yourself into the future, envisioning yourself at a very old age. Get into the feeling of having lived out your days and being close to physical death.

- As this old person, look at the picture of yourself at midlife.

- What do you notice about this person?

- How does this person look physically?

- What do you remember about what this person's concerns and problems were at this age?

- What would you say to this person if you could speak to him or her from where you are now in time?

- What advice would you give to this person, knowing what you know now?

- Now return to your present self.

- What insights have you gained from seeing your younger self and your older self?

- How can you integrate those insights into your present life?

Aging creatively will engage all aspects of our human existence, and that's what it takes to move forward. Being creatively engaged in what we are meant to do allows the inevitability of the aging process to take its natural place in our experience, nothing more, nothing less. Neither avoiding nor clinging to the process of aging frees up a great deal of time and life force energy to engage in what our Genius spirit points us toward. Creative aging allows us to include all aspects of our lives in our great life experiment, leaving nothing out. From this expanded vision which includes both limitation and expansiveness, loss and gain, regret and opportunity, we live as more evolved and dynamic human beings who are capable of embracing the amazing gift of earthly life.

8

The Gift of Disillusionment

Many years ago, while visiting the Getty Museum in Los Angeles, I came upon a painting by Swiss painter Ferdinand Hodler entitled *The Disillusioned*. I remember seeing this distraught figure of a barefoot man dressed in robes sitting on a small wooden bench. His brow is wrinkled, and his eyes are wide open and cast down, as if to suggest a mixture of worry and defeat or some terrible truth having been realized. His expression communicates the weight of responsibility thrust upon a person who has suddenly and simultaneously had the ideas of himself and the world razed to the ground. The responsibility this painting implies is that of continuing with his life somehow without the slightest idea of how to move forward. This task includes feeling the pain of the past while embarking on a new life chapter, which can be viewed as the existential mandate of being able to remember what has happened to us while dreaming of what our futures could be simultaneously.

Oddly, I remember actually feeling quite optimistic at seeing this painting. It was a strange feeling at the time, as the painting clearly depicts an older man in a state of total despair. I think the word *disillusioned* was what was revelatory to me, as it pointed to the fact that one's illusions being taken away can make one sad and despondent initially, but a less precarious and illusory life is being heralded by this very same occurrence. I had not yet reached midlife at the time but nevertheless received the message that there were challenges to come that would strip the illusions I had had of myself and of the way I regarded the world, making way for a more expanded viewpoint and depth of understanding. Little did I know that I would one day take this man's place, sitting on the little wooden bench, eyes cast down, worried and wondering what the hell I was going to do next.

A definition of the word *disillusion* is "to free from or deprive of illusion, belief, idealism, etc.; disenchant." Most of this phrase sounds quite positive — it contains the words *to free from*, which suggests a previous state of bondage or imprisonment from which one is released. This kind of incarceration is within the shackles and bars created by beliefs and idealism, which can be the strongest prison of all for keeping a human being locked away. The word *disenchant* in this definition comes from the Latin word *incantare* which means "to enchant, or fix a spell upon." Part of being disillusioned is therefore is to be freed from an enchantment or spell under which we have been living. The spell of identifying with a form of a psychological prison is broken, and we realize that we are now responsible to break free from our self-imposed limitations of beliefs and ideals that no longer serve us and can take us no further in life.

Our basic ideas about ourselves, or our *schemas*, serve as a platform for our very personality and ego, and without them we feel hopelessly lost and helpless. Allowing them to change into newer and more appropriate ideas that support our current lives is usually facilitated by an experience of great disillusionment, and this is a completely natural and healthy phenomenon. But allowing them to be changed is similar to undergoing surgery without anesthesia and subjecting ourselves to the surgeon's work without resisting or getting in the way.

Such a surgery and a realization is an initiatory rite of midlife. We don't realize how we got here, but we know for sure that something on a basic level of our identity isn't working any more. It is at this point that we have a choice to make. We can either attempt to maintain the status quo and cling to the ideas, ideals, and identifications of our younger years, or we can allow the natural tide of human life to carry them out to sea. If we hold on to the ideals of our past, we are out of step with life and will continue to suffer. If we let these identifications go, through conscious awareness and regardless of how bitter the separation tastes, the space left by their absence becomes fertile ground for the emergence of a new life schema or identity, which includes the deep knowledge gleaned from our past experiences along with a new world full of possibility existing outside the walls of the old prison. We can begin to dream of the future again and of things that were previously impossible from behind the bars of our old, worn-out identity.

Again, rediscovering Genius is the perfect avenue for this identity transformation. Getting back to the roots of our individualism through creative play and expression is a way of turning the soil of our consciousness so that the seeds of possibility that are present there have a chance to sprout. Making an environment within ourselves that is conducive for our Genius traits to emerge and express is what this opportunity is about. Our Genius qualities and talents are underutilized and important parts of ourselves, and now is an auspicious time to bring these gifts to the foreground. At midlife, it takes a disillusionment to clear the way for a more rewarding existence that can be filled with work that is satisfying, relationships that are built on mutual respect, and a general gratitude for the wisdom of the universe, which has obviously been guiding us without our knowledge all along.

Midlife Crisis vs. Midlife Opportunity

Nearly every adult in the Western world is aware of the idea of midlife crisis. The concept is woven into our modern cultural mythology as a phenomenon which happens to men and women between the ages of 35-53 and is usually evidenced by a reversion to an earlier pattern of behavior more befitting a 20-something version of themselves rather than what may be expected of someone in their 40s. The actual term *midlife crisis*, introduced by Jaques in his 1965 paper entitled "Death and the Mid-Life Crisis," refers to a period he describes as beginning at around age 35, when a crisis develops around the identity of an individual and lasts for a period of years before having the possibility of being resolved in older age. In his paper, Jaques proposes three possible paths of individuals considered to be creative Geniuses by midlife and the different outcomes these paths can lead to. One thing that all three paths have in common is that the midlife period presents unique psychological challenges that can break or transform an old identity or reveal and bring to life a new one with which to encounter and navigate the world.

When the word *crisis* is replaced with the word *opportunity*, the meaning goes from experiencing a chaotic change of events, to which we basically have no choice but to succumb, into a set of circumstances presenting an opportunity for change and growth. This middle-stage-of-life phenomenon can thus be reconsidered as a *midlife opportunity*. A midlife opportunity is experienced by both men and women and is more related to the suppression or expression of our Genius qualities than simply a struggle with our existential identities. What is at stake in a midlife opportunity is the development of a human quality that can allow the space, time, and circumstances for the Genius spirit in us to either emerge, if it hasn't yet, or to expand if it is presently being expressed in some form.

Sometimes, all it takes to make a shift in our focus is to shine a fresh light on our situation, and this can begin with the language that we use to describe the thing that is happening to us. Exchanging the word *crisis* for the word *opportunity* may seem to be a simple exercise in optimism or a psychotherapeutic reframe, but instead, it can be a revolutionary transformation of our perception. The important difference lies in our willingness and ability to focus on either the end of something or the beginning of something new, on either the past or the future, on death or potential.

At the midlife stage, we are confronted with this choice of focus, and one need not be merely an optimist to choose to focus on the potential for growth when given an opportunity. We can simply observe, regardless of how tentative our current situation may be, that there is still much life left to be lived: our unique life, which is not over yet. When we give credence to our Genius qualities, we carry a responsibility for whatever time we have left to express these talents and gifts.

What is it to be responsible for expressing our Genius traits? The word *responsibility* comes from the Latin word *respondere,* which means "to respond, answer to, and promise in return." To be responsible to our inbuilt Genius is therefore to respond to it calling to us. The first step is to acknowledge that the Genius spirit actually exists, that it is an intrinsic part of us, and that it is wanting to express something. The second step is to answer the Genius in us by making time and space for this expression to occur, realizing that we are suffocating an extremely important part of ourselves if we don't allow a path for it to manifest. The third and possibly most important of all of the attributes of responsibility is to promise in return. This is the transcendent part of the Genius way. We approach our Genius with a sense of the sacred in whatever way suits us. We return the promise of Genius to enrich our lives with a promise of our own to include it in our life expression. This promise is not a religious vow or a dry discipline but rather a conscious intention we set to remain open to the expression of this unique part of ourselves into the world.

Urgency

One dynamic of life that I have witnessed time and time again is that when we dare to take one step forward toward a goal, the earth suddenly appears underneath our outstretched foot to support our step. Movement begets movement. Participation on our parts sets a universal dynamic into motion, and life responds in kind.

When we take a step toward the expression of our Genius, things that are literally impossible to imagine will appear in our lives to help us out. The collaboration with our Genius wants to happen, and it will respond to our efforts to locate it. Instead of waiting for our Genius to arrive and tell us what to do, we can take a leap of faith in the form of taking a single step in the direction of its expression. This leap of faith may look like buying a canvas and some paints or running an ad online offering our unique services to others. It could manifest as looking into returning to school or planting a garden. Anything that is an attempt to feel our way through the foggy landscape of midlife uncertainty is a statement of our intention. This deliberate movement on our part raises the level of urgency and creates the need for the Genius spirit in us to respond. The more we move toward Genius, the more it moves toward us.

The following story is an illustration of having the right kind of urgency; one that comes from our innermost heart that cries for our authenticity as unique individuals living in the world.

There is an old story about a certain mystic who was fond of borrowing money from lenders and, in turn, giving the money to local religious institutions and humanitarian causes. It came to pass that the mystic became gravely ill and was on his deathbed. All of the people to whom he owed money had shown up in a last attempt to collect on his debts.

The mystic clearly had no money, much to the consternation of the lenders present in the room. The mystic called for some refreshments to be brought for his "guests." A young boy selling halvah was called in from the street, and his supply of this sweet confection was distributed around the room. When the boy asked the mystic for payment, the mystic replied that he didn't have the money to pay him. The boy, who was obviously very poor, began to cry bitterly, knowing that his boss would surely punish him for the lost income. Just then, a messenger appeared at the door bearing a generous donation from one of the mystic's benefactors, enough to pay off all of the mystic's creditors as well as the halvah boy.

The mystic explained: "In order to facilitate this occurrence, a genuine need had to be involved. A true urgency came in the form of the boy needing to pay his boss. The lenders who are present here today have plenty of money, and their need was strictly a business transaction. There was nothing desperately important in their requests. The boy's need represented life and death to him. His desperate condition raised the right kind of urgency that the universe responds to and will always answer.

From this story, we can glean the questions we need to ask ourselves at midlife:

- Have I uncovered the right kind of urgency?
- Does my urgency indicate a need to be aligned with the lost and unexpressed part of me?

- Can I use my disillusionment and confusion as something that will move me forward on the road to the discovery of my innate Genius?

Luckily, these are questions that we all must answer for ourselves. I say "luckily" because the answers we will find will be our own. On this part of our life journey, it is our individual responsibility to listen to what our hearts are saying, rather than accepting others' ideas about who we are. The answers will come from paying close attention to our inner and outer experiences once we have begun the Genius quest. Our observations will guide us on what steps we will need to take next.

From birth, we are bombarded with ideals and concepts of who we are supposed to be. Many of us never manage to climb out of this readymade identity that has been imposed by our given name, our family's religion, and our culture with its mores and norms. However, by midlife many of us are feeling the urgency and need to discover something uniquely our own. This feeling is a gift of the Genius spirit in us that continues to call us to express our unique talents and share our individual gifts with the world.

The Genius turns up the heat at midlife, the urgency being that time is running short for us to express ourselves and live as uniquely expressive individuals. The urgency is deeper than a selfish need to show off and be seen as important by being different. It comes from a genuine and universal desire that has been with us from birth to express our one-of a kind Genius. In this respect, the most personal of experiences, that of a unique expression of oneself, isn't personal at all. Its inception occurred at an existential level. We are an expression of existence itself, and it is existence that wants to emerge, manifest, and express itself as the unique individual we are. We're just along for the ride.

While the past-facing ego in us is desperately trying to make its mark on the world, our Genius already contains a blueprint for our unique expression. As time goes on, the urgency to allow this expression becomes greater, since there may be a lot of ground to cover in a shorter time, depending on how much we have allowed our Genius spirit to emerge as an active part of us. If we can see and feel this urgency of the Genius expression as a natural urge, like hunger or thirst or relationship and belonging, we would be sure to give ample time during our day to explore and express it.

Like eating, drinking, and breathing, creative expression is a basic need of human beings. It has been so through millennia and in every culture, and only recently has it been consigned to the back pages of our syllabus as an elective activity. If we have ignored the need for creative expression due to the idea that it is impractical or unnecessary, it is as if we are living an oxygen-deprived existence, with all of its accompanying symptoms.

Genius Deprivation Syndrome

If we look at what happens to the human brain from oxygen deprivation, we know that in most cases, brain cells begin to die after 1 minute of no oxygen supply, and after 3 minutes of not breathing, our bodies usually die altogether. This is a very small window of time to be without an essential, life-sustaining element before some kind of permanent damage is done. This fact also suggests that we are interdependent beings that count on a myriad of conditions continuously occurring for us in just the right way and in the correct proportions. These conditions are provided for us so consistently that they go generally unnoticed and unappreciated. Air, water, light, darkness, and the functions of the immune system and other bodily systems are all freely provided and performing perfectly without taking any credit or demanding our acknowledgement. As human beings, we also have the need for meaning and purpose. We can fool ourselves into thinking that these are merely electives or low level priorities, since their absence doesn't kill brain cells or lead to physical death. But meaning and purpose, which are the products of making space for our Genius expression, are intrinsic to our inner lives. Fortunately, if we discover that we have been Genius-deprived and that a part of our interiority has died, we can activate the phoenix-like nature of consciousness that resurrects itself from the ashes of our previous identities. We may carry the experience of our youthful selves having died from a lack of creativity and personal expression, but when we acknowledge our Genius spirit and give it room to move, we are born and live again regardless of how dark and deep our graves have been.

Symptoms of Genius deprivation syndrome may include:

- weak libido or life force
- depression
- anxiety
- feeling stuck in an unrewarding job or career
- feeling that something important is missing from your life
- feelings of purposelessness and lack of life meaning

The need for Genius expression in midlife has never been greater. Our genuine callings are seeking expression through us, and if we continue to deprive ourselves of them or to confuse their signals to us with some sort of illness, we will continue to suffer. Since it is natural to want to put an end to our suffering, we can thank the uncomfortable feelings associated with Genius deprivation syndrome for being a motivating force for lasting personal change.

Character

The uncovering and expression of our Genius qualities is not a guarantee of fame, recognition, or worldly success. These things are what Lao Tsu calls "the flowery trappings of the Tao" and can serve to confuse our understanding of what is essentially important about expressing our innate Genius. Recognition or success may or may not occur; it depends on the particular gifts that our Genius has come to bring to the world. Instead, Genius is about experiencing a sense of purpose, meaning, and fulfillment that has more to do with living from our unique character and inner integrity than it has to do with worldly recognition of our individual brilliance.

The root of the word *character* is traced back to the Greek work *kharakter*, which was an engraving tool. The word was used as a metaphor, as a mark, symbol or imprint on the soul. Character is also considered as comprising the defining traits and qualities of a person, or someone's distinctive nature. Our character is our inner refuge and home; we use it as our individual palette of colors in painting the portrait of our lives. Genius is the artist that uses our character to create and express.

By the time midlife has come, our character has had time to develop through both our inner and outer experiences. It has been shaped by the ways in which we reacted and responded to what has appeared as challenges to us in our lives. These challenges have all been opportunities presented to us as instruments of potential inner growth and development, and we have either accepted or declined them in various degrees along the way. Luckily for us, it seems to be the nature of the universe to continue to present opportunities to us for continued growth and development of character. It seems to want us to get the point of certain specific life lessons that are meant to deepen and enrich us by making an imprint on our souls.

> "Talent develops in solitude, character develops in the stream of life."
> — *Johann Wolfgang von Goethe*

Since each of us has unique Genius qualities to express and develop over time, it would seem that the central focus in our lifetime would be to bring out those qualities and that to miss the opportunity to be who we were meant to be would constitute a major life failing. Our individual character therefore depends on uncovering our own particular Genius seed and letting it grow throughout our allotted time.

> *Zusya was a well-respected and devout Rabbi who had lived a long life of spiritual service to his community and students. On his deathbed, his students found him weeping and crying, tears streaming down his face. One of his students, knowing that Zusya's time was near, asked him, "Zusya, why are you crying so? Are you afraid that when you meet God he will ask you why you weren't more like Moses in this life?" To which Zusya replied, "No, I am not afraid to be asked why I was not more like Moses. I'm afraid that when God sees me he will ask me why I was not more like Zusya!"*

Many teaching stories, like this one, use the image of impending death as the metaphor for the urgency for change. Impending death casts a light on the rest of our lives like nothing else can, and the perspective it can provide allows us to sort out the essential from the nonessential. In this light, we can see the importance of love, given and accepted; of honesty to ourselves and to others; and of being the genuine expression of ourselves, regardless of what it may look like to the world. When we are faced with impending death, we have no time left for things that ultimately don't matter.

The realization of our mortality is a common occurrence at midlife, and we go through the stages of grief related to losing the false sense of immortality and invulnerability that it was necessary for us to have in our earlier years. When we finally reach the stage of acceptance, and at this point I'm speaking about the acceptance of our eventual death, we have the ability to summon this sobering awareness when we are faced with difficult and trying situations and experiences. The gift of the realization of certain, eventual death brings with it a scale with which to measure the essential as opposed to the inessential in any circumstance.

Deathbed Exercise

Summon the idea of a difficult situation or decision that you are currently facing. Hold the image of that situation or decision gently in your awareness. Now imagine that you are at the end of your long life, lying on your deathbed, surrounded by loved ones, and from this vantage point, look closely at that current challenge.

- What is at stake in your current situation?
- What can you actually do exactly right now to address it?
- Is this issue essential to your life expression or is it something that can be let go?
- What overall importance does this issue have to you from the perspective of your death bed?
- What things, if any should you be focused on instead?
- Notice any other insights you may have received from this experience.

Take the time to acknowledge the answers that you came up with in light of your impending death, and see if there is an overarching theme that has been uncovered. Take this theme as a tool for your decision-making process in the here and now of your life.

Accepting our mortality is also instrumental in uncovering and developing our character. The acceptance of what simply is provides a weight and substance to our life expression that changes our basic perception of things in our lives, helping us weigh and sort them into essential and nonessential categories and saving us the precious time and energy needed to uncover and express our Genius qualities while we still live.

I have a longtime friend name Billy who was a fellow spiritual seeker and business partner to me throughout my entire adult life. Throughout the years, we have become more like brothers than friends. A few years after we both got married later in our lives, we dissolved our professional ties and went our separate ways. Billy and his wife bought a house and began to remodel it themselves. One day, as Billy was guiding a subcontractor who was driving a delivery truck onto his property, he momentarily turned away from the truck. The driver, not seeing that Billy was behind the truck, stepped on the gas pedal and backed over him with the rear wheels of the truck. Although Billy actually survived, his body was crushed, and he suffered a head injury, broken legs, arms and ribs, internal bleeding and memory loss. He spent months in the hospital and years in physical therapy to regain the ability to walk. He literally lived through being run over by a truck.

When I speak to him these days, rather than anger at the truck driver or self-pity for his more limited physical mobility, Billy expresses gratitude for his life. He is acutely aware that he could have easily died under the wheels of the truck that day. In the light of his experience, he has lost a great many of the fears of hospitals, operations, physical pain, and suffering that he had been carrying his entire life. The buoyancy that he experiences comes from going through hell and returning to see that life itself is what matters — not pain, fear, or worry about the future, but life in its immediate and present moment. This is what Billy now naturally expresses as his character.

We need not have a life-threatening accident to uncover and develop character, but we do need to digest the lessons of our experiences in the light of our certain mortality in order to get to what is essential. At midlife, we have the choice to complain and bemoan the fact that we are getting older or revel in how young we still are. We can cling to the idea of physical youth, or we can gracefully embrace the natural movement into older adulthood that carries with it the advantage of not having time to waste on nonessential things.

Either/Or vs. This/And

To actually continue to live consciously through and past midlife, we will need to develop the capacity to invite necessary changes to our consciousness through seeing things as *this/and* rather than *either/or*. We have already mastered the art of seeing things in terms of being good or bad, right or wrong, or, in other words, the tendency to engage in black-and-white thinking. What is needed for a successful midlife transition is a departure from this kind of unconscious habit. And it can be an extremely stubborn one to break. But break it we must if we are serious about moving ahead with our midlife expansion.

Black-and-white thinking is something that begins at a very early stage of cognitive development. It is an easy way for infants and young children to define what they like or dislike. It also helps them to categorize things into one of two opposing categories in order to fulfill as well as possible the still-forming ego's need to control and predict events that may happen. Not moving beyond this type of thinking as adults makes us practitioners of avoiding pain and chasing happiness. This is a fear-driven mentality that breeds an us-versus-them psychology as well as extremist thinking. Politicians use this tactic to their advantage when framing an issue. The direct message of "if you're not for us, you're against us" is an example. This message requires a perceived dilemma in order to work effectively, like creating an enemy of a person or group of people in order to have something to be either for or against. This practice of appealing to people's black-and-white thinking is also used by various news organizations in order to push their particular politically motivated agenda onto their viewers.

As we age, however, experience shows us that life experience exists on a spectrum. Nothing is completely black or white, good or bad but instead contains a measure of each. The demarcation lines are blurred. A tendency of those who are stuck in the either/or stage is to dwell on the negative aspect of things in an attempt to protect themselves from potentially unpleasant or harmful experiences or perceived dangers. But this tactic only helps to attract more negativity. Paradoxically, it also "protects" them from experiencing more positive experiences. Seeing things as existing on a continuum allows us to see that bringing our focus to what is actually working in our lives, while acknowledging what is not working can result in a transcendental vision that brings a third perspective of our situation that always surprises us when it appears.

The Transcendent Function

By midlife, most of us, to some extent, have the uncomfortable awareness that our life experiences and conditions are neither good or bad but contain elements of both simultaneously. We can see the advantages and disadvantages of living out our lives, having to make decisions, and dealing with their consequences. Through dealing with this paradoxical quality of life, we may have gained the capacity to be able to make room for these two seemingly conflicting yet equally valid realities happening at the same time. We may have ended a long-term relationship due to consistent difficulties that we just couldn't work out with our partner. This breakup brings a sense of relief from not having to experience the frustration brought on by our difficulties. But at the same time, we deeply miss the things that did work between us and our partner that were equally as real and brought a sense of fulfillment and belonging to our life. So what can be done with these conflicting feelings? How do we learn, integrate, and make use of them?

Jung developed a theory that takes into account this paradoxical quality of life. His idea is that we make an inner space within our psyche large enough to hold the *tension* that these two conflicting and opposing emotions create inside of us. By consciously holding space for the natural tension created by these two emotions, we are giving our psyche a chance to deepen and embrace the paradox instead of choosing one option or the other. When we can allow the realities of both things to exist without choosing, we are allowing a third, unexpected thing to emerge in our conscious experience. Jung calls this capability of the psyche the *transcendent function*. This phenomenon brings a resolution to the tension that we've been holding by bringing forth a solution that otherwise we could never have foreseen or created by reasoning or logic. This resolution becomes evident in the expansion and deepened capacity of our consciousness to live with paradox. It makes mystics of each of us by somehow magically transforming us into individuals who have transcended black-and-white thinking regarding the experiences we have lived through.

The awareness gained by the transcendent function at work in our lives brings out realizations that can be compared to having birthed a child. A child is the result of two opposing forces coming together to make a third thing. The aggressive sperm and the still and receptive egg coexist long enough to produce something that is made up of both but is also completely individual. The child that we have created by making enough space to hold the tension of two opposing feelings is our deepened and more nuanced awareness, and is a living paradox for which we become responsible to nurture by allowing it to be expressed through our actions into the world. This is the way we change. This is the way that we flourish in midlife; by living the truth of our deepened inner experience in thought, word, and deed.

The third thing that is produced through the transcendent function of the psyche can be seen as one of the greatest gifts that can be given to anyone. This phenomenon actually changes us in a way that nothing else can. When our conscious awareness is changed by a psychic revelation, transcendent in its nature, we ourselves are changed. This type of change is incredibly rare and precious. This change can redefine and resurrect the parts of us that have become stagnant and stalled through the unconscious repetition of behavioral patterns in our younger lives.

Older people are said to be "set in their ways" only because they have been unwilling to let go of what they have known and believed to be true in the first half of their lives, and that unwillingness begets the stiffness and atrophy of what was once alive with new possibility in them. They have become "set" as in concrete or stone. They exist more like statues than as living and breathing human beings. Statues can represent something that once was; a memory.

We have the unique opportunity at midlife to see more clearly what is individually most important to devote our time to. Having invariably wasted and used a lot of it up by now, how we spend our time has become increasingly more important to us. All of us have always had an unknown and limited quantity of time granted to us from the start, but we are more aware of this fact at midlife than someone still living under the spell of physical youth. By holding and making inner space for all of the opposing feelings we have about how we have lived our lives up until now, the transcendent function can take place and present us with a new vantage point from which to embark. For the first time in many of our lives, we can really focus on living from what our experience has shown to be genuinely necessary and important to us as individuals. No longer bound by the need to follow other's ideals out of the lack of or distrust of our own, we can create the life that we actually want to live instead of living as drifters who move from one thing to another due to the absence of trust in ourselves as individuals.

9

The Contract with Heaven

Ancient Chinese culture, as did many other ancient cultures held a belief that there exists a basic agreement or contract between each individual human being and Heaven. This, as any contract is an agreement between the two parties, with each party expected to fulfill their portion of the terms agreed upon. This contract with Heaven is considered to be an individual's mandate for the way in which they live their life, the things that they are expected to do, and who they are destined to become.

In this belief, as with the concept of the inbuilt Genius spirit, Heaven or the Universe provides each individual with their own unique storehouse of qualities and talents sufficient to allow them to fulfill their part of the contract on earth. The individual's part of the contract is fulfilled by first uncovering their cache of unique callings and qualities given to them in potential, and then to use these provisions to express something uniquely individual outwardly into the world. In this way, the individual is a conduit of the Universe's unique expression of something it wants to express on earth. An interesting part of this belief is that a person's general health and wellbeing is tied to how much they made use of their storehouse of gifts. Lonny S. Jarrett, a Doctor of Chinese medicine writes:

> *"Heaven plants the seed of original nature within and from the moment of the first breath attempts to nourish that seed at every opportunity. Humans by rejecting their life circumstances and ignoring their internal mandate separate themselves from all that is truly nourishing in life"*

So to consider the collection of problems we may face at midlife as symptoms of ignoring our part of our contract with Heaven means that our healing can take place by turning our attention to the particular gifts given to us as part of our original nature and by making an effort to bring those qualities into expression.

The idea of fulfilling one's part of a contract, especially a contract with Heaven means that the effort we make to do so is completely supported and encouraged by existence itself. So the effort we make to discover and embrace our authentic lives carries with it the full cooperation and help of the Universe. IT wants us to bring out our unique qualities just as much as we want to express them. We are not alone in our task; we have an extremely wealthy benefactor who has a vested interest in the completion of our work.

Of course, we have the right to ignore our innate callings and not fulfill our side of the contract. But remember that finding and being true to the gifts we've been given is what brings deep meaning to our existence like nothing else can.

Reevaluating Our Past

Because of the tendency at midlife for us to become aware that the first half of our lives have already been lived, to whatever degree of satisfaction or disappointment, the time that has passed may appear as an epitaph on the gravestone of our youth. Instead of experiencing our past as a valuable foundation or platform upon which to build the rest of our lives, we may feel limited and stuck, living with the results of the choices we made during that time. The "reality" of what has taken place before seems actually to be written in stone, and it can feel like we're carrying that stone around our necks. There seems to be little possibility of moving forward with such heaviness weighing us down. Due to the nature of our memories to change over time and the human tendency to exaggerate and embellish the memories of events that have had the greatest impact on us, we owe it to ourselves to reevaluate and re-vision our past experiences in order to give them fresh meaning in the context of our current awareness.

From the vantage point of midlife, we can take a look at the events that we have experienced before and how we were changed by them and assign them new meaning. Guided by the wisdom gained over half of a life, we can see things now that we couldn't possibly have seen before. We can imagine all of the choices we have made over the years as beads on a necklace that we are now wearing. The individual beads, seen as a design on the necklace, each have their own place in the arrangement, which makes up a whole piece of jewelry. Although they were originally individual choices and experience, on the necklace they are seen as one, unified thing.

Many of these "beads of experience" represent a wounding that occurred as the unexpected result of a choice or experience we lived through. A wounding always calls out to be healed. We can address this need for healing by revisiting our wounds from the perspective of midlife and actively see them differently than we had seen them before; we can see them as events that occurred in a pattern over a long period of time. From this matured viewpoint, they may appear differently due to the total or sum of our life experience. Things that once were seen as misfortunes may now, in the light of experience appear as blessings, and things that were seen as fortunate may in hindsight be seen as a curse. In observing our past in this way, we are actually changing it by allowing ourselves a fresh understanding of it. We are not changing the events, but rather our perspective on them as seen in the light of how they fit together as the expression of our youth.

If you were bullied at school when you were a child, for example, you can look at how part of your personality was formed because of the way that particular wounding took place. You can see how your reactions to it have shaped your behavior over time. You may observe that you have become more empathetic and sensitive to the suffering of others. Or you may have developed a tougher ego in order to deal with the world's cruelty. You may have forgiven the other child for his or her actions toward you, seeing them now from your adult perspective as childish behaviors, or you may still carry a grudge and hope that the person has been punished for his or her treatment of you as a child. Some of our motivations that stem from our early experiences and choices are serving our current lives in a positive and productive way, and others are not. Since our aim is to move forward in a creative, expressive, and holistic way, it may be time to bring a fresh perspective to our view of the past in order to release the energy it takes to continue seeing it in the old way.

A small treatise attributed to a 7th-century Chinese sage named Seng Ts'an speaks about seeing things from a vantage point he refers to as *the way*:

> *When the mind exists undisturbed in the way*
> *Nothing in the world can offend,*
> *And when a thing can no longer offend,*
> *It ceases to exist in the old way.*

Midlife is the time for the shedding of the old ways of seeing that no longer work for us.

Whatever our current mindset about our past experiences, seeing them through the lens of our distilled experience of the first half of our life can help us to revision and reevaluate their value to us going forward. As Seng

Ts'an says, when our memories of the past can no longer can offend or trigger us to react to them, they cease to exist in the old way, or rather, we cease to exist as our old selves who seemed to have no choice but to react. By applying the insight that is available to us at midlife to our old psychological complexes, we can change our current life experience; thus, the reality is that we can significantly change our experience of life by changing how we view our past. That view will not change by denying how our experiences have affected us but rather by their integration into the totality of our life expression. Good or bad, painful or pleasurable, all experience serves to deepen and enrich us as individuals.

Giving space for our Genius to emerge more fully into our life expression can directly affect how we see our past and thereby produce change in the present. Our Genius traits, especially by midlife, will creatively use our experiences as the artistic materials with which to express themselves. We can imagine our sufferings and victories as paints in various colors from which the Genius can choose to do its work. The more varied and deep the colors are, the better. If part of our Genius is to sing, then our experience of gain and loss can come through the quality of our voice. If our Genius expresses itself through doing volunteer work, our personal experience of needing help at one point will translate into compassion for others. If one of our Genius gifts is to mentor others, understanding our wound from the lack of a responsible, caring parent can translate and be expressed as a deep and compassionate care for others.

When we see how our past experiences are used creatively by our Genius qualities to express something new and unique, we may find ourselves feeling a sense of gratitude for everything that has taken place in the past. As we discussed before, this is not an *either/or* sense of gratitude whereby we dismiss any pain we have experienced and lopsidedly try and replace it with gratefulness but rather a *this/and* gratitude that makes use of and integrates the whole spectrum of our experience as important and irreplaceable. Genius has the capacity to change the way in which we perceive ourselves in the present, which in turn can literally change our past in terms of how we conceive of and value it. By allowing the perceptions of our lives up until now to change, we free up an enormous amount of psychic energy that had been used for keeping our old feelings about our past intact. Don't be surprised if you feel a creative surge as a result of letting go of the old way of seeing things. This surge of vital energy, or libido life force is one of the things that we felt was missing at midlife, and we were right to feel incomplete without its presence.

Our calling

A dream of finding our calling in this life is one that most people have. We dream of feeling solid and secure in our decision-making regarding our vocations and careers. We feel as if we would respond with the conviction of Noah if we heard the call from God or the Universe and would live a rewarding, fulfilling life from doing what comes natural.

For many of us in midlife, the original blueprint we designed based on what we perceived as our true calling has been reduced to a wrinkled and torn piece of paper that once bore the plans for a mighty palace. Through the years, it has gone through revision after revision; the ballroom removed here, the atrium taken off there, the ceremonial gardens forgotten and abandoned due to our storehouse of enthusiasm having been drained away. Because of our life's challenges and disappointments, and from our personal failure to bring this palace into being, our blueprint for something unique, meaningful, and fulfilling may have been forgotten. Or our palace on the hill may have changed to a house in the suburbs simply due to a failure of imagination.

Calling is a very misunderstood idea by most. We hear stories of people who listened to their calling and went on to experience great adventures because of what they heard. There were also those who didn't respond to their calling and ended up living a life punctuated by feelings of disconnection and disappointment. Most of us live in the latter of these two conditions and, by midlife, feel that our opportunity for following our true calling has come and gone. Meanwhile, we have succumbed to a societal status quo where all we can look forward to is a well-earned retirement and a minimum of suffering as we reluctantly slide down the other side of the hill toward death.

Pretty grim description, I know, but luckily for us, true calling has a dimension to it that is largely beyond our awareness. In terms of our unique Genius, the purpose, meaning, and talents it possesses never go away and never lose the requisite amount of enthusiasm and imagination to manifest its expression into the world. In other words, from the Genius perspective, our calling continues to call to us throughout the entirety of our lives.

As Westerners, most of us have embraced our culture's penchant for being self-starters as well as its expectation of us to use the "pull yourself up by your bootstrap" qualities of individualism. We may have retained only a dim, pre-societal childhood memory or sense that there is another dimension to this calling thing. Wouldn't it be great if our calling is actually drawing us to it as much as we are trying to get there by ourselves? Couldn't we use that magnetic force that was attracting us to our particular vocation as a source of energy and inspiration?

Living Teleologically

The ancient Greeks had a word that will assist in this explanation of calling: *teleos*. This word was used by philosophers such as Aristotle to mean "end, goal, or purpose." Aristotle's idea was that everything in creation is moving from an imperfect state to a state of perfection. Just as an acorn contains the blueprint for an oak tree, moving from potential to manifestation, we contain the Genius seeds of the perfect expression of who we actually are in potential. Looking at our lives *teleologically* is to see that each one of us is being pulled toward becoming a perfect specimen of what we are destined to be.

We are born as seeds of something greater. Sadly, many of us live our entire lives as seeds, never responding to our natural growth progression and, consequently, never unfold into our mature form. A seed is not meant to live as a seed; its purpose is to grow into something else. If it doesn't fulfill that purpose, it stagnates and rots. This unlived potential is one of the causes of sadness and depression and manifests in our lives as a myriad of symptoms, affecting us mentally and physically.

By becoming aware and responding to our innate Genius, we can participate with the teleological journey we are here to undertake. The ingredient that has been missing in most of our experiences is that we feel that we are alone on this endeavor and that our struggle to become what we actually are occurs in our own personal vacuum. This is far from true. Our struggles to germinate and grow are being witnessed by our Genius spirit, and Genius is pulling us toward our potential as much as we are struggling to get there. An acorn has the potential of the oak tree inside of it, but it must go through the necessary steps in order to become one. Our struggle to encounter and express our Genius qualities can be seen as our willingness, like the acorn, to be planted underground and go through the process of germination. We will need to turn within ourselves and be quiet in order to listen for the next clue. What happens next for the acorn is that within its dark and damp earthen enclosure, it splits open. We go through necessary crises where we experience cracks in our identity in our dark phases. The acorn next experiences something extraordinary: something entirely new and unexpected grows from the crack. Something mysterious and green moves from within it and upward toward the surface. From the cracks that have appeared in our old identity, new and unique qualities emerge that are beyond our dreams, and they start to seek expression in the world. From the dark, the acorn sends a shoot upward toward the light, and it breaks the surface of its darkness to express a form: a sprout that, although similar to other sprouts, is completely unique in its expression. We begin to show a quality of ourselves that may feel strange at first but expresses itself outwardly nonetheless. Its expression is unique, one of a kind, and will never be expressed in this way by anyone else, ever. The acorn sprout *is* the oak tree. If it continues to grow, nature will help to nurture and feed its evolution naturally. Our first natural expression of our Genius is our Genius. And the same forces of nurturance and care are at work. Genius has a vested interest in our growth and maturation.

When we enter the Genius journey, it is not as an isolated pilgrim, but as a child belonging to a great cultural lineage and tribe who has been greatly missed and who is on his or her way home again. Although we can be said to be fortunate if we express our Genius in this life, we are actually fortunate because of the Genius that resides in the DNA of our consciousness. It is a genuine quality and ingredient that each of us has in the marrow of our being, like blood, like bone.

> "Every substance not only possess a form; one could say it is also possessed by a form, for it naturally strives to realize its inherent form. It strives to become a perfect specimen of its kind. Every substance seeks to actualize what it is potentially."
> — *Richard Tarnas*

10

Water Artistry

"Under heaven nothing is more soft and yielding
than water. Yet for attacking the solid and strong,
nothing is better; it has no equal. The weak can
overcome the strong; the supple can
overcome the stiff."

— Lao Tzu, Tao Te Ching

One way to illustrate the way in which we can allow our
Genius spirit and qualities to emerge is with the image
of water. In many places on the earth, by simply digging
deep enough, we will find a source of water. If we move far
enough into our own depths, we will find an essence that
embodies water's qualities. Its natural tendency is to move
and flow, changing shape and direction when needed.
Anything that can flow can overcome obstacles it encounters
in its path by virtue of its innate nature. It does so
effortlessly, because this is what it was born to do.

We can all uncover this water-like quality by
approaching our lives as artists. In seeing our everyday
experiences with Genius eyes, we can respond to them in the
present moment in a creative way. Using the palette of our
Genius' character allows us to create and express what is

natural for us as individuals. The more we practice from this unique and one of a kind source of creativity, we are making more space for our Genius to emerge and make its contributions to the world.

The greatest piece of art is a life well lived. If you are reading this, there is still time to allow a rich and fulfilling life to emerge. Listening to our Genius' callings enables us to respond to them artistically, with a sensitivity and deep appreciation for what is wanting to be expressed. As artists creating our own lives, our priority is to uncover our inbuilt qualities and talents and bring them into the world through whatever type of expression comes natural to us.

The Art of Enjoyment

It doesn't matter how good or fortunate someone's life is unless they have developed the capacity to enjoy it. At midlife we may have accomplished and acquired various things that are not currently making us happy. This is not the fault of the accomplishments but rather an indication that we have a problem with our basic ability to enjoy them. It would seem that it would take an effort to learn this ability, but like the Genius within us, it simply needs to be uncovered; the capacity is already there. Creating a practice of enjoying things can open up a deeper dimension of our lives. In the following story we can see an example of how this practice can look.

> A certain man was walking near the edge of a cliff one day, when suddenly the ground beneath his feet gave way. As he was falling, he grabbed a tree root that was protruding from the Cliffside. As he was hanging suspended there, he noticed a large tiger below him who had seen the incident and was pacing back and forth in anticipation of a meal. Above him he saw that two mice had arrived and were chewing through the root he was

holding onto. Unable to move up or down, he was
frozen with fear and dread. Just then, he noticed a
strawberry growing on a vine from the side of the cliff,
just within his reach. He spontaneously decided to reach
out and pick it. It tasted so sweet!

One aspect of this story, told in various forms and in many traditions, illustrates our capacity to find a way to enjoy what is presented to us in each moment. Almost without exception, the present moment in which we find ourselves is generally okay. We can see this when we gently separate out the thoughts and worries about what is going to happen in the future from what is immediately available to us.

In my therapy practice, I work with a good number of clients who experience depression. One of the symptoms associated with depression is cyclical negative thinking; the imagination is being used to blacken any possibilities of a positive future. Regardless of what I may suggest, many clients are quick to point out the impossibility of anything ever making a difference in their lives again. Even though my therapeutic approach is to honor the symptoms of depression and listen to what these symptoms are asking for, I sometimes ask my clients to focus on one single thing that is actually working for them right now, such as noticing how their breath is going in and out of their lungs effortlessly without them having to do anything, or that they are actually able to speak incredibly well about feeling so terribly bad. For all of us, this practice is not an attempt to ignore or repress the difficulties we face but instead to include genuinely good and positive experiences, however small, that are happening alongside the difficult and painful ones in the pantheon of our human experience. To deny that depression is difficult and painful to move through would be untrue, but denying that some things do work well is equally false. At midlife, having lived through both easy and difficult times, we are now capable of holding more ambiguity and nuance in our daily experience instead of seeing things as black or white, or all good or all bad. We can accept that at any given time, there are easy and difficult things existing side by side in the moment-to-moment experience of being human.

Regardless of our present state, our Genius and all of its resources are available to us when we acknowledge it and invite it to express itself. Genius qualities don't wait until all of the clouds have parted in the sky of our consciousness and for the sun to be shining through them. Genius can use every part of our life circumstances as a starting point for creativity and expression. It effectively removes any excuses that we use to postpone living the purposeful and meaningful lives we would like to live. The question then becomes whether we are willing to let go of our excuses and get on with it.

Moving Forward

We can only move forward with our lives once we have let go of our attachment to what has happened before and what the past has made of us as individuals. We have been affected by our experience in various ways in our earlier lives, and midlife is a perfect and crucial time to step back, take a deep breath, and examine what we are currently holding onto from the past. Most of us cling to the experiences that have wounded us and made us hyper-vigilant against them ever happening again. Operating from a sense of fear of past experiences repeating in the future will certainly prevent us from embracing our future potential. Moving forward means that we are ready to start a new chapter, and that requires beginning with a fresh, unwritten page.

The term *tabula rasa*, which translates as "blank slate," is usually used in reference to the notion that we are all born as blank slates, empty and impressionable, and that our experiences become written upon that slate and make us who we are as individuals. The Genius way can be seen as different from this concept in that we come to this life with our Genius traits and talents intact, and we are not simply an accumulation of experiences over a period of time. When I mentioned a new chapter in our lives needing a fresh page, I wasn't suggesting that we start again, empty-headed and childish, but rather as experienced and nuanced individuals who are armed with the insight of what we have learned from the past. Like our Genius traits, our experiences have become distilled into qualities of our character. We can trust that this priceless distillation will be there at our disposal even if we stop clinging to it. And we will need to stop clinging to the past in order to move forward into the potentiality that awaits us.

How do we turn the common midlife realization that we only have a limited amount of time left in our lives into a sense of enthusiasm for the future? In a 1959 interview, this dilemma was addressed by Jung, whose creativity, intellect, and sense of adventure lasted his entire life, even after a heart attack at age 68. He said,

> I think that it is better for . . . [an old person] to live on, to look forward to the next thing as if he had to spend centuries, and then he lives properly. But when he is afraid, when he doesn't look forward, he looks back, he petrifies, he gets stiff, and he dies before his time. But when he is living on, looking forward to the great adventure that is ahead, then he lives.

Here, Jung is speaking about a basic dynamic of consciousness. Simply put, when we live looking forward, as if life will continue, our lives will be open to new adventures and possibilities. When we live looking backward, however, we are living outside of the vital stream of conscious awareness that always moves with the present. Living this way, we are as good as dead, because we're living only as defined by our past experiences. We become stiff and unmovable, brittle and breakable. All that it takes to switch to moving forward in the present is a willingness to let our past be put in its proper perspective by life itself, whose nature is to go on.

The example of a snake illustrates this point. A snake has to shed its skin, its exterior, which has been used for a certain time while navigating through his environment. His skin has served as a protection and a home, borne his wounds and scars, and has developed a distinct history. But after a while, a snake will naturally leave his outer skin behind because a new layer of skin has grown underneath that is intended to replace the old layer. In order to survive and move forward with his life experience, he has no choice but to discard it. If the snake were unwilling to undergo this releasing of the old, the possibility of his agile movement would be limited; he would become trapped in his own past, due to his defense against potential loss. But time and time again, the snake's experience is that something new comes to replace the old. In fact, it is the new skin growing underneath that sets this change into motion in the first place.

Consider the snake's new skin as part of his Genius qualities. When the perfect time comes, his Genius creates an expression of new skin that is destined to come to the surface. If the snake ignores this natural occurrence and tries to cling to his old, outward shell, he will suffer from going against a natural phenomenon that is much deeper and stronger than his fear of losing what he is. All the snake needs to do is to allow the Genius' impulse to emerge, and the old skin will fall away of its own accord.

The key here is to recognize that we have naturally occurring processes that are regularly trying to replace our old, worn-out perceptions with new ones that will serve us better moving forward. The blessing of free will may turn into a curse if we exercise it to leave the stream of life that flows endlessly on and instead sit on the bank at one point and build our house there. At first, it may feel like we're creating something solid and stable, a protection against the elements that life consistently throws at us. But the Genius in us is always moving, creating, and responding in the flow of life's stream. Our Genius lives in the stream, and not on the bank. When we've chosen to live on that bank, it's not strange that we feel uncomfortable when the Genus qualities in us are trying to pull us back into the current of life in order to have some new and fresh experiences. It calls us to risk the outdated ideas of ourselves against a new vision containing our unlived possibilities.

Experience as Wealth

One of the many things that are obscured during the struggle of the midlife period is the value of lived experience. Without exception, those of us who have lived until midlife have had their share of success and failure, heartache and happiness, and have succumbed to and overcome difficulties and challenges and somehow managed to keep on living. There is nothing on earth that can give us such a great amount of vital information as having lived through something. The trouble comes when we ignore the hard-won battles and the lessons learned because they don't seem to help us in our current situation. Underestimating the value of mistakes, seeing regrets as an unending hell, and skipping over our large and small victories without acknowledging and reveling in them all point to what Socrates called an "unexamined life." Invariably, it is the things that change our perceptions of ourselves and the world that have the greatest importance and make our experiences a treasure trove of incalculable wealth that we carelessly carry in our hobo sack on the end of a stick.

If we are to turn our situation around at midlife, our effort is to recognize that all of our experiences, whether we deem them good, bad, or mediocre, have deepened us and given us character, untapped strengths, and wisdom. Midlife is the time to call upon these experiences and the ways we've reacted or responded to them to come to our aid as light-bearers illuminating our path forward. We have paid dearly to be where we are, regardless of whether or not we value our present situation. We have paid with a portion of our limited and unknown amount of time here on earth to be just right here, just as we are. In short, it is time to take stock of what we have gained and lost, what we have learned so far, and what we have yet still to learn.

Viewing our experiences from a Genius perspective, we will see that all of them are worthy of our compassionate examination. Even those that are a source of shame and regret can inform us further, if we can suspend our judgment of them just enough to recognize the import of the lessons we have received.

Self-Mirror Exercise

One way to recognize the value of our experiences is to do this exercise to see yourself as a different person sitting across from you in a room. This person has had the exact same experiences as you have and has been affected by them in the very same way. This is your mirror self.

- Sit across from an empty chair and imagine your mirror self is sitting there.

- You are aware of what that person has been through and experienced in their life. They are asking you what they should do right now to help themselves to live more fully and authentically.

- You may want to give this mirror self a name; speak to them using your insight into their life to help them to see their situation more clearly.

- Address their concerns and fears, and point out their strengths and inner qualities that they have developed that will help them to navigate their current challenges.

- Explain the great potential that you see in them to overcome their difficulties and encourage them to use this potential in their daily life.

- Give them specific examples of how they can do so.

- Remind this mirror self that at any time, you can have this dialogue with them to clarify their current situation, and continue to move forward.

Surprising the Stars

There are many times in our lives when we are presented with extremely difficult circumstances that we somehow are forced to face and to deal with. Most times we don't feel that we actually have the strength or depth of energy that we need in order to navigate what's been put on our path. The fact is that part of the dynamic of human life is made up of and will always include the challenges that come from the changes that occur in our lives.

Although life changes are often chaotic, disruptive, and even destructive, they are serving a specific purpose. They are designed to actually show us hidden strengths that we are completely unaware of that we actually possess. These strengths can only be activated by a deep necessity on our part; by a genuine existential emergency, which presents us with a choice. This moment of choice is extremely poignant and irreplaceable. At

> "When we are no longer able to change a situation - we are challenged to change ourselves."
> — *Victor Frankel*

this crucial moment, when we are on the threshold of choosing either to expand past our limitations or to remain small, the entire universe is witnessing us with bated breath. It has no idea what is about to happen. Existence itself is waiting to be surprised by the mysterious and creative power of free will that we possess. And when we choose, in that amazing, sparkling moment to expand our depth and understanding, to step outside of the old way of seeing things, we change the entire quality of the universe we live in. We may not know where we're going, what we're doing, or who we're becoming, but we can sense that we have just taken a step on a path filled with new beginnings, possibilities, and potential.

Midlife will certainly provide many challenging opportunities for us to grow and change, and sometimes it won't look pretty to begin with. But remember that in order for a seed to grow, the soil it gets planted in must first be disturbed and overturned in order to make a place for the seed's potentiality. Life changes disturb the very ground of our limited existence in order to make a place for the greater flowering of our experience, allowing our roots to grow deeper into the earth while our branches and leaves reach further towards the heavens. When we can embrace the challenges that we are given with an open heart and a willingness to change, our inner strength and creativity increase dramatically, and we are blessed with a vision of our current and future selves that could not have otherwise become visible to us.

Going forward, your lives have not been written in stone. There are great possibilities ahead when you use the time you have on this earth to become your authentic self. Miracles and mysteries can and will happen. Now go out and surprise the stars.

ABOUT THE AUTHOR

Ben Hummell is a Licensed Professional Counselor and a Marriage and Family Therapist. At the age of nineteen Ben was drawn to the practice of meditation and dedicated himself to a life of spiritual discipline and the goal of enlightenment. He found himself teaching spirituality and helping to guide other spiritual seekers on their individual paths at an early age. The combination of his youthful enthusiasm, idealism, and a genuine spiritual calling fueled the path throughout his 20's, 30's and 40's. During those 30 years, he was a Spiritual Counselor, Public Speaker, Entrepreneur, Woodworker, and Musician.

At the age of 49, Ben found himself in the midst of a difficult life transition; a spiritual disillusionment and loss of faith had lead him to yet another search for identity, life meaning, and purpose. After years of disorientation, confusion, and struggle, he came to learn about the ancient concept of a Genius spirit that is born with every individual – a life-guiding force complete with talents, abilities, and a genuine calling to a unique expression of one's gifts. His research into Genius helped Ben to realize that one of his Genius traits had always been to help others to navigate difficult life transitions and encourage them during that process.

Ben's professional training is as a Depth Psychotherapist, which means that his approach to helping others through difficult times always takes Soul into consideration when addressing the issues that his clients bring to their sessions. His work with others is also strongly influenced by his 36 years of meditation practice, which has developed into an ability to work with others with depth and wisdom.

Ben offers private and group therapy sessions in Ashland, Oregon as well as individual Genius Coaching sessions by phone or on Skype.

Essential to Ben's approach is the idea that the uncovering of one's Genius continues throughout the entirety of life. He has seen that many pivotal changes and resolutions to problems can take place in a person's life by uncovering their unique Genius talents and embodying them actively in the world.

Keep up to date with Ben
on his website here:
www.BenHummell.com